ESSAY ON DIVORCE

AND

DIVORCE LEGISLATION,

WITH SPECIAL REFERENCE TO THE UNITED STATES.

BY

THEODORE D. WOOLSEY, D.D., LL.D.,

PRESIDENT OF YALE COLLEGE.

NEW YORK:
CHARLES SCRIBNER AND COMPANY.
1869.

APPENDIX.

TABLE OF CONTENTS.

PREFACE.

THE following Essay is a reprint of articles which appeared in the *New Englander* for 1867 and 1868, with a number of changes and additions, among which latter the notes at tho end of the volume are the most considerable. The work was undertaken, not from any special interest in the subject, but from a sense of its importance; and the author had been urged for a number of years to write upon it, before he found time to give it any thing like due attention. The call which came to him was dictated by a feeling, in which multitudes share, that the Divorce Laws of the State where he resides are extremely lax, and that a commonwealth, whose morals and history in the past have been highly to its honor, is in danger of becoming a teacher and propagator of low views of the marriage relation, as far as its example can reach. The call came to him because he had studied the subject in connection with lectures on Natural Right and the State, delivered in Yale College, and was supposed to have some familiarity with the exegesis of the New Testament. How he has done his work the reader must judge.

As for the treatment of the subject the author wishes to say :—1. That the multitude of details, especially in the fourth and fifth chapters, is so great that he cannot expect to have avoided mistakes, and as all the books that were consulted were not at hand for re-examination, the errors could not be conveniently detected. 2. In the last chapter it might seem as if he was inconsistent with his own principles in allowing cases of divorce which are condemned by the greater part of Christian people; but in truth the remarks that are there made are dictated by the conviction that a strict law would not stand any chance of being passed in a number of the United States. If however a law as good as, with one exception, that of England is could be accepted in this country, no one would rejoice more than the author.

PREFACE.

Several gentlemen have rendered valuable assistance to the author in regard, especially, to the state of Divorce Legislation in the United States. He mentions here with gratitude the help given by Henry Clark, Esq., of Rutland, Vermont; Rev. W. W. Andrews and C. J. Hoadley, Esq., State Librarian, of Hartford, Conn.; Edward D. Mansfield, Esq., lately Commissioner of Statistics in Ohio; H. W. Chase, Esq., of Lafayette, Ind.; S. B. Perry, Esq., of Chicago, Ill., and Henry Hitchcock, Esq., of St. Louis.

New Haven, *March* 31, 1869.

ESSAY ON DIVORCE.

CHAPTER I.

DIVORCE AMONG THE HEBREWS, GREEKS, AND ROMANS.

In the present chapter we shall attempt to give an account of the law and practice of divorce among the Hebrews, Greeks, and Romans, those three nations, to one or another of which we owe our religion and most of the leading elements of our civilization. The subject has an important practical bearing. It is intended as an introduction to an inquiry into the meaning of those passages in the New Testament where the matter of divorce is taken up. Christ, by a few words on this subject, has turned legislation and usage into a new channel; he has in those few words, by a higher conception of marriage than was entertained before, thrown in a very important element into Christian civilization. It is our object to answer the question why Christ acted thus in some sense as a legislator, and what the world's need was that it should be taught a higher morality in this respect. Having looked at this point as briefly as truth and the importance of the subject will permit, we propose, in the next chapter, to discuss the passages of the New Testament touching on divorce and the questions to which they naturally give rise. Then, if it is permitted to us to continue our inquiries, we shall treat of the practice and views of the early Christians, and of the state of opinion and law in some of the principal Catholic and Protestant countries. Finally, we shall ask what ought to be the aim of legislation among us, and how the Christian Church ought to act in endeavoring to enforce the commands of Christ within its own pale. Our aim is to do good and to serve the truth. We are not indeed so conceited as to hope to produce a great effect of ourselves, but believing that an irreligious liberty is creeping even into the Church with regard to the marriage tie, believing also that nothing more helps on, and is helped on by, general laxity of morals than undue freedom in regard to divorce, we feel constrained to contribute our mite to the correction of a public opinion and practice which are threatening serious evils both to Church and to State.

DIVORCE AMONG THE HEBREWS.

The ideal of marriage, as we find it in the first records of the Hebrews, is a peculiarly beautiful one. "For this cause shall a man leave his father and his mother and cleave to his wife, and they twain shall be one flesh." Here the union of one man with only one woman is thought of, and polygamy in fact is inconceivable, for how can so close a union as the being one flesh with a wife admit of the same union with another. It is again an indissoluble union; for if the parties are one flesh, nothing but a violent process of nature or of crime, something like amputation, can separate them. And what is deserving of equal notice is the separation of the man from his father and mother contemplated in this text. A patriarchal age would naturally regard the filial and parental as the closest of all ties. Here is a still closer tie, involving a greater "cleaving" to the wife, a formation of a new family with new rights and interests, an emancipation from parental control.

The ideal presented in these words remained in the Hebrew mind until Christ came into the world. Polygamy and freedom of divorce obscured, but could not obliterate it. Polygamy was permitted or rather endured, under some restrictions, but one wife was the rule, as is shown by various passages of Scripture. In the Psalms, and in the Prophets, only one wife is spoken of; the prophets are nowhere mentioned as having more than one; the same is true of Moses and of Isaac; even Abraham looks forward to the necessity of having a servant for an heir, until at the instigation of Sarah he takes Hagar as a kind of substitute for her; wealthy men, like Nabal and the Shunammitish woman's husband, are monogamists; and perhaps the law laid down a similar rule for the high priest.* Probably a great part of the private persons among the Jews had but one wife, and polygamy was chiefly confined to the king and a few others. Even the kings were forbidden to multiply wives greatly, and Jehoiada, the high priest, must have intended to restrict King Joash, when he furnished him with only two. Still polygamy existed legally, and was not put down by the moral sense of the nation. It took, we may add, through the prevalence of slavery, the form of a looser connection with a woman of inferior condition, a form between concubinage and marriage. The woman in Judges, chapters xix., xx., is constantly called a *pillegesch* or concubine, and yet the Levite is spoken of as her husband, and her father as his father-in-law. She was a Hebrew free woman apparently, but that relation, for the most part, was entered into with a domestic or a slave.

Marriage began with the betrothal, but no covenant or formality is known to have existed. The condition of marriage, however, is spoken of as a covenant. Thus Malachi says: "Yet is she thy companion and the wife of thy covenant;" and Ezekiel: "I sware unto thee, and entered into a covenant with thee, and thou becamest mine."

* This opinion, thrown out by Saalschütz (Mos. Recht., p. 748, ed. 2), will not bear much weight.

In numberless instances the word *zanah*, to play the whore, is transferred to signify a breach of the covenant-relation between God and the people by the crime of idolatry. Closeness of union and tender care, conditioned by fidelity, belong to both relations, that between husband and wife, and that between God and the people. Did the notion of a covenant belong to both independently, or was it transferred from the theocracy to family life? We are unable to give a satisfactory answer, but apparently it originated in the theocratic union and passed to the conjugal. However this may be, there is a sanctity thrown around marriage by this manner of speech and thought, such as few other expressions could give forth. If adultery is on a level with apostasy from God, how great must be its guilt; and if the man is to the woman as God to the people, what but a breach of that covenant in one vital respect should dissolve the union. To which we may add that as God had but *one* people, the standing simile would be apposite only if, as a general thing, one man had but *one* wife; and that the relentless severity of the Jewish law toward the adulteress corresponds to the penalties it denounces against going away from Jehovah to the worship of a false god.

In Hebrew marriage, gifts were given or a price was paid by the bridegroom, and this corresponds to the purchase of the wife, which was practiced over a large part of the world in ancient times, as in Greece, among the Hindoos, and among the Germans, and of which many instances are still to be met with in barbarous or half-civilized tribes. In the first case where these presents are spoken of, the largest share went to the bride, Rebekah, her mother and brother also receiving "precious things." In the case of Jacob, as he had nothing to pay, service was rendered as an equivalent. The other references to this usage are few; fewer, we conceive, than they would have been, if it had played the same important part which belonged to it in the marriage usages of other nations. A distinguished writer on Jewish antiquities tries to show that the custom among the Jews amounted to nothing more than the giving of presents for a favor received, which presents went in good measure to the bride; but the prevailing opinion is against him, and the analogy of other nations is able to show a softening down of an original purchase from the father into a portion conferred upon the bride herself.*

Hebrew marriage, thus far, appears quite informal and primitive, but yet penetrated with a religious spirit, and placed, as it were, under the especial protection of the covenant-keeping God. Nevertheless as the bad usages of polygamy, slavery, and blood revenge were endured among the people, so when it received the law, a freedom of divorce prevailed which could not be corrected

* We refer to Saalschütz (u. s.), chapter 102, § 3.

without hazarding the overthrow of the polity. It was therefore endured, and in some degree restricted.

The leading passage relating to divorce is found in Deut. xxiv. 1–4. It assumes a certain loose practice in regard to divorce, and tries to reduce it to a formal shape, precisely as the Emperor Augustus attempted to give legal form to divorce among the Romans by his legislation. Let us notice the parts of the passage in their order.

1. It is supposed, as the basis of the law now given out, that husbands who had found "some uncleanness" in their wives had been in the habit of putting them away without ceremony, or of sending them home as they would hired servants. Here two things deserve consideration. *First*, the right of divorce among the Hebrews was altogether one-sided. The wife had no right of divorce whatever. If her husband committed adultery with a married woman he might be put to death; but it does not appear what protection she had against ill-usage on his part. Probably her vindication in this case was left to her friends. In the second place, what do the words "some uncleanness" denote? This passage, as is well known, was the subject of controversy between the schools of Shammai and Hillel: the latter understanding it of any thing offensive or displeasing on the part of the wife; the former giving it an ethical sense, according to most modern writers, as if it were to

be confined to an act of immorality like adultery. Winer, however, says that the Gemara makes the view of Shammai less strict: even public violations of decorum might furnish ground for divorce according to his doctrine. Josephus interprets the law according to the views of Hillel: "He who wishes to be separated from his wife," says he (Antiq., iv., 8, 23), "for any reason whatever [St. Matthew's 'for every cause']—and many such are occurring among men—must affirm in writing his intention of no longer cohabiting with her." This is the extreme of license which an immoral age would defend by the passage. On the other hand, the opinion attributed by most modern writers to Shammai is wholly untenable, as moral uncleanness or adultery was punishable by death. Knobel, in his commentary on Deuteronomy, expresses himself as follows: "*Ervath dabar* is used of human excrement in Deut. xxiii. 13, and is properly a *shame* or *disgrace* (Is. xx. 4) *from a thing*; that is, any thing which awakens the feeling of shame and repulsion, inspires aversion and disgust, and nauseates in contact, for instance, bad breath, a secret running sore, etc." Then he adds, "in the time of Christ the expression was in controversy. The school of Shammai took it as being the same with *debar ervath* [a thing of uncleanness or disgust], and understood it of unchaste demeanor, and shameless lewd behavior. The school of Hillel, which the Rabbins follow, explained it as *something disgusting or any other cause*, and thus defended a looser view . . . . . Both were wrong in this, that they built up a general principle upon the words, whilst the author only speaks of the commonest cause of divorce at his time."

2. It is required of the husband, by this statute, that he write a bill of divorcement, and give it into the hand of his wife, before sending her away from his house. The law requires no special form for this "writing of separation," and whether any form in particular was customary we have no means of knowing. The essential points which the law aims to secure are first *a formal writing*, by which any passionate haste would be prevented; and secondly, *protection for the woman*, so that it should appear to all persons that she was not an adulteress, nor a runaway from her husband's house, but was free to contract a second marriage. If the reasons for the divorce were added in the bill this would be an additional protection to the wife, as the husband would be slow to put down in a permanent form pretexts which might be false or frivolous.* It has been suggested also that at an age when writing must have been infrequent, the inability to prepare a written document would secure a greater degree of deliberation, as the husband would need the help of some Levite or other educated person, of whom he would stand in a

* In the forms given by Selden, Uxor. Hebr., iii., 24, no mention is made of any reasons.

certain awe, if conscious of the frivolity of the reasons for a divorce.

How far this statute went into general use, we have no means of knowing. Two passages, one in Isaiah (l. 1), and one in Jeremiah (iii. 8), refer to the bill of divorcement to illustrate God's treatment of his rebellious wife, the people, and as the illustration must have been well understood, it is fair to suppose that such bills were then in common use. The passage in Jeremiah however suggests a difficulty. God put backsliding Israel away and gave her a bill of divorce on account of her adultery. May we argue from this that the penalty of death for this crime was now softened down, on account of the great corruption of manners, into repudiation. The passage in Ezekiel (xxiii. 45, 46), where judgments by righteous men in cases of adultery are spoken of, proves the contrary. Jeremiah adapts his simile to the facts of the case. The adultery of Israel was the abandonment of Jehovah for the idols of the heathen, and his repudiation of her was the captivity of the northern tribes. The very verse of the prophet where these words occur shows us the freedom of his illustrations. The treacherous sister of Israel, Judah, feared not when she saw the casting out of her sister, but went and played the harlot also. Here then we have two sisters contemporaneously the wives of one husband, a thing directly against the law of Moses.

3. The divorced wife may now contract marriage with another man, but if separated from him by death or divorce may not return to her first husband. As Jeremiah says the land where this should occur would be "greatly polluted." Here protection for the woman and for public morals are secured at once.

As for the woman, the great freedom of divorce which law and usage gave to the man made it all the more important that her interests should be protected. She was always the passive party, having no right of divorce on her side. If such freedom on the part of the man was right, it was right also that she should be permitted to marry again. If it was in itself an evil, endured but not encouraged, it was in a certain sense right that another similar evil should counterbalance it and deprive it of some of its baneful effects. Marriage ought to be equally sacred for both parties, and under equal sanctions for both. When there is a letting down of those strict rules which our Lord has made known for his Church, bad law cannot end, with any equity, in granting the husband certain liberties, unless it grants a compensation to the wife. This compensation was remarriage after divorce. The need of such protection was increased by the institution of polygamy, for it would often happen that the husband, when he took to himself a second wife, would become disgusted with the old one, and her feelings, when she felt herself to be put in the background, would not contribute to domestic peace. Or he might find himself unable to support two, and thus disgust would ere long end the connection with one of them or the other.

As for the protection of public morals, it is evident that the power of return to the same husband might wholly destroy the sanctity of marriage and bring it down almost to the level of *polyandry* on which a few of the most degraded nations of the world now stand. Marriage between one man and one woman must be once for all. That is to say there is nothing in the mere act of divorce, according to this Hebrew law, to prevent reunion of the parties, and very likely such things occurred, but a practical dissolution by marriage to another man forever prevented a union with a former husband, as something polluting and almost adulterous. So enormous a transaction as that between Cato the younger and Hortensius, when the former lent his wife Marcia to the latter and took her back again after the orator's death, would have been altogether contrary to Hebrew law, and probably an abomination to Hebrew feeling in the worst times.*

It is only seldom that the law of Moses makes mention of divorce. The two other passages where

* It does not appear that Cato ever divorced his wife, which only makes the transaction more enormous. For a critique of this affair, see Drumann Gesch. Roms., iii., 107.

it is spoken of, show an intention of a humane legislator to protect a woman in circumstances where she was peculiarly exposed to injury. One of these is Deut. xxii. 28, 29. The substance of it is, that a man who deflowers an unbetrothed virgin, besides paying a fine to her father, shall take her for his wife without the power to "put her away all his days." The other (vv. 13–19 of the same chapter) contemplates a newly married man's spreading an evil report concerning his wife's antenuptial chastity. If on solemn investigation it was found that his words were false, he was to be chastised, to pay a heavy fine to his father-in-law, and, as in the former instance, to have his liberty of repudiating her taken away. In these cases the interests of morality and those of his wife are both looked after. Yet it may be asked whether such a law, implying a grievous breach between the married pair, would not expose the wife to intolerable cruelties from one who could never get rid of the detested object. We can only answer that the law allowed no such cruelty, that her family friends could act as her defenders, and that on his death she could not, it is probable, be stripped of the use of some portion of his property.

We have no means of judging whether the sentiment of the Hebrews changed in the course of time on the propriety of divorce. There is, however, one memorable although very obscure passage in the last of the prophets (Malachi ii. 11, 16), which goes to show that indiscriminate divorce was then regarded by good men as wrong and offensive to God. The prophet, after rebuking intermarriage with heathen women, and threatening the divine vengeance against those who should commit this sin, passes on to a second sin, that of "covering the altar of the Lord with tears, with weeping, and with crying out," which, as appears from the next verse, where the sense is more fully brought out, is to be understood of the complaints of injured and divorced wives—divorced perhaps for the sake of the heathen women just before spoken of—uttered in the temple to the Lord of Hosts. God no longer regards the offerings of such men, because they have dealt treacherously or unfaithfully each one against the wife of his youth, who is his companion and the wife of his covenant. The next words are among the obscurest in the Bible, and if we could make them plain, they would require too long a comment for this place. Then the prophet adds: "therefore take heed to your spirit and let none deal faithlessly against the wife of his youth. For the God of Israel saith that he hateth putting away, for one covereth violence with his garment, saith the Lord of Hosts." The marginal rendering of our version—"the Lord God of Israel saith, if he hate her put her away," which was given by Jerome and adopted in Luther's Bible, would now have, we suppose few defenders. Ewald's version (in his Prophets) follows the Septuagint in making the sentence conditional: "when one out of hatred puts away, saith Jehovah God of Israel, he covereth his garment with violence." In this version no good sense is elicited; the rebuke against divorce in the preceding context is not confined to cases where the husband hates the wife; and the conditioning clause which this rendering assumes is strangely divorced from the conditioned. Hitzig in his commentary translates: "he hateth putting away, saith Jehovah (i. e., Jehovah saith that he hateth), etc., and him who covereth wrong with his garment;" Köhler, a more recent commentator (in his Prophets after the exile, part 4), "for I hate putting away, saith Jehovah, etc., and crime covereth his garment" (who doeth this); DeWette in his version: "for I hate putting away, saith Jehovah, etc., and him who heapeth crime on his wife." Nor is Hitzig reluctant to adopt the translation *wife* instead of *garment* at the end of the passage.*

Hitzig well remarks on the passage, "that the putting away of the wife was indeed permitted (Deut. xxiv. 4), but was not on the whole a thing which God could look on with complacency, and in the case before us it had in it something hateful, not merely on account of its frequency. Perhaps we have here the beginning of the stricter doc-

* A condensed exposition of this passage is given by Keil in his Commentary on the twelve minor prophets, not long since published. He adopts Köhler's views in almost all cases.

trine of the New Testament." The beauty and noteworthiness of the passage consist in the deep moral and religious feeling which pervade it. The wife and husband are bound by a covenant. To put a wife away is to break that covenant, to act treacherously or faithlessly. This is what God hates. We have thought while studying this passage how our Lord must have pondered over it, and how two places of the ancient scriptures, one at the beginning, one at the end, coincide with his views of divorce, while the law and practice of the Jews spoke only of the hardness of their hearts.

It only remains to inquire what was the usage of the Jews through their history, and a very scanty answer is all that can be given. What the moral sense of the nation allowed when the law was given is gathered, as we have seen, from the law itself. This passage of Malachi goes to show that even in a reformed age, among the returned exiles, the practice of divorce was not infrequent. Examples however do not occur. In the time of Christ it must have been not uncommon, although nothing can be argued in regard to the morals of the nation from Herod the Great and his family. Josephus tells us (in his life, §§ 75, 76) that he was thrice married. The first wife and he separated. He does not tell us how or why. The second he put away, "not being pleased with her character," after she had borne him three children. Then he took a third, whom he praises highly. The probability is that multitudes of his countrymen, especially the more heathenish part of them, made no scruple of dismissing their wives at pleasure.*

DIVORCE AMONG THE GREEKS.

There is a great contrast between the destinies of the conception of marriage as it appeared in the Hebrew mind and in the Greek. In the former race, most beautiful and elevated at the outset, but long encountering inveterate oriental practice, and failing in a great measure to be realized, it is at last purified and brightened by Christ, so as thenceforth to enter into the thought and life of the world. Among the Greeks, on the other hand, simple and severe at first, as it was among the other western nations, averse to polygamy, perhaps regarding divorce with disfavor, this conception became obscured and degraded as they advanced to the acme of refinement. The mythology which was elaborated in the earliest epic period by the poets reflects already the morals of a corrupted race, for they who could listen eagerly to rhapsodists narrating the adulteries of Zeus or Hephæstus, must have been defiled themselves, and must have grown more so from famili-

* The authors whom we have principally relied upon are Saalschütz (Mosaisches Recht), Selden's Uxor Hebr. in Vol. II. of his works, Winer's Realwört., and leading commentators. Selden, from the mixture of the Rabbinical and scriptural, is very wearisome and confusing.

2

arity with such examples. Still a simple unsensual mode of life, and original tradition guarding the sacredness of the family union, may have in part for a long time counteracted the influences of mythology. But when we come to the historic ages of Greece, the case is widely different. At Sparta, notwithstanding the severity of the institutions, the sanctity of married life was not respected. It was reputable and customary there for men to give over their wives to their friends, and a king, for reasons of state, was allowed to have two wives in two separate establishments.* At Athens, the maid was reared in seclusion to protect her from the evil without. She thus became an unfit companion for the man who enlarged his mind by taking part in public affairs. Was it strange, when as a matron she came to have a larger liberty, that she should abuse it? Or was it strange that the *hetaera*, conversant with men and used to please men, should usurp the wife's influence? But it was strange, sadly strange, that the corruption seized on youthful beauty as its instrument, that a frightful unnatural crime, punished with death in Christian lands, fastened itself on the intimacy of older with youn-

* See what Xenophon, in his Lacedemonian polity near the beginning, says of this and of a still more disgusting practice, with no reprehension, and ascribing the licenses to Lycurgus. This scholar of Socrates can have had no moral but only a political view of marriage.

ger men, and if not without rebuke, yet swept abroad so widely, as to be the greatest disgrace of the Greek civilization. The study of morals and the revival of moral feeling in the schools of the successors of Socrates could not stem the corruption.* The later Greeks of the Macedonian and Roman periods, if we judge of them correctly, were more enervated, more immoral, where they had opportunity, than before, both outside of Greece and within it. Marriage came to be regarded only as a convenience or as an evil; population fell off; whatever Greek virtue of the political sort had existed in great measure left the race.

Aristotle remarks in his politics that the old Greek laws and usages were very simple and barbaric, and gives us an illustration that they carried weapons habitually, and bought their wives from one another. This custom of purchasing the wife, of which we found traces among the Hebrews, sprang out of the view of the child as the property of the parent: the father had a right to the services of his daughter until she passed beyond his control. This usage is often alluded to in Homer. The word for the purchase-money is *hednon* or *hedna*, but inasmuch as the word may have had the wide sig-

* Beautiful passages in Plato's Laws show that he was awake to the importance of purity in the family relations. A passage in the eighth book, where he would have law attempt to secure in the new city a degree of purity which he regards as almost chimerical, is well worthy of notice (p. 841, D).

nification of a gift or present at first, and as the father would naturally give a part of this wife-money to his daughter as an outfit, it occurs also in the sense of a present from the father to the daughter, and in that of a present from the betrothed man or from other friends. Thus an epithet applied to maidens can be translated *cattle-finding*, because by the husbands whom they won they procured cattle for their fathers. So also it is said of a Trojan ally who was slain by Agamemnon, that to obtain his wife he first gave a hundred cattle, then promised a thousand head of sheep and goats besides. Sometimes the father waived his right of purchase-money for his daughter; Agamemnon is willing, if he can propitiate the angry mind of Achilles, to give him either of his three daughters without getting any *hedna* on his own part, and he will give large presents in addition. When a wife had been unfaithful to her husband, he could claim the price he had paid for her; and when for some other cause he had put her away, he was expected to pay back the amount of the gift or dower granted to her by her father. These usages may have differed little from those of many other nations.

In Sparta, after betrothal, marriage was consummated by a kind of mock robbery. At Athens betrothal was universal in legitimate marriage, and a dower regularly but not necessarily went with the bride. She might have none, and yet be a lawful wife, whereas under Roman law the dower was so much more essential, that the civil law has been thought to entertain a presumption against marriage without dower as being no more than concubinage. That religious ceremonies attended the marriage festival is undoubted, but no public priest's services can be shown to have been thought necessary. As women and children were always minors at Athens, the wife passed from under her nearest relative, as her *kyrios*—her guardian or law representative—into the hands of her husband, who sustained the same capacity. Yet it may be added that as parental power was not so extensive at Athens as at Rome, so it was with marital power also. After the death of the husband or the divorce of the parties, the wife fell under the authority or guardianship of her next blood relative.

Divorce at Athens was easy and frequent. It took two shapes, distinguished often by different words, being called *sending away* or *out of the house* (*apopempein* or *ekpempein*), when the husband repudiated the wife; but *quitting and going away* (*apoleipein*) when the wife separated herself from her husband.* In the first case, little if any formality seems to have been required, although we may perhaps argue from the instance of a leading Athenian mentioned by the orator Lysias, that the husband usually made known his intentions before witnesses called in for that purpose.

* Other terms also occur, as ekballein, apoluein, aphienai.

There are several instances of this kind of divorce mentioned in the private orations of Demosthenes, which demonstrate what a bare matter of convenience marriage was at that time, and how destitute of a moral element. Timocrates, having found a rich heiress with whom he could connect himself, sends away his wife, who without the interval of a day is married to Aphobus, one of the guardians of the orator Demosthenes during his minority. Protomachus, a man in needy circumstances, having the same chance, persuades his friend Thucritus to take his wife from him ; her brother betroths her to this second husband, and the plaintiff for whom the oration is written is her son. In a third case, Polyeuctus adopts his wife's brother, gives him his own daughter for his wife, and then, some quarrel having arisen between the parties, takes her away and gives her to Spudias. Then a suit concerning dower was brought by the former husband against the father and the new husband. In this case, if Leocrates and his wife did not agree to separate, the latter must have initiated the steps for the divorce, for it nowhere appears that the father or previous *kyrios* of a married woman possessed this power. In all such cases, notice in writing of the divorce was probably lodged with the archon or judicial magistrate.

The other description of divorce was when the wife left her husband,—when she began the proceedings. In this case, she was required to appear in person before the archon at his office, and there present a writing in which the reasons for her separation from her husband were set down. If both parties were agreed about the divorce, that might be the end of the affair. She returned to her nearest relatives, and her husband was obliged to pay over any dower that might be in his hands. If the parties were not agreed, a suit might arise, and the same seems to have been true when the husband began the proceedings, but nothing is known of the judicial process in either case.

It was when Hipparete, wife of Alcibiades, and daughter of one of the first men at Athens, stung by the outrageous licentiousness of her husband, had gone to the archon to take the above-mentioned legal steps for a divorce, that Alcibiades collected a band of men and dragged her away from the place of justice. He may have done this for the sake of her great dower of twenty talents. At all events, according to Plutarch, he quashed the proceedings, for she lived with him until her death. The same writer adds that the law required the presence of the woman desiring a divorce at the place of public justice, in order that it might be in the husband's power to come to terms with her and keep her with him.

Suits were doubtless very frequent in regard to the wife's dower, which was either paid over to the husband before witnesses or retained by her *kyrios*, subject to the stated payments of interest. If paid over, security was taken on her behalf upon her husband's property, and he was also bound personally for it. If he delayed to pay it over after the divorce, eighteen per cent. yearly interest was due for the time of the delay. More might be said on this matter, but the legal consequences of divorce do not fall within our subject. It is needless to add that she was free to marry again as soon as the divorce took effect.

We have confined ourselves chiefly to Athens, partly because it is a fair sample of the more modern civilization of Greece, and partly because the materials are exceedingly scanty, or fail altogether, for the greater number of the Greek States. Legislation, however, made various experiments. We give one example. Among the laws of Thurii in Magna Græcia, according to Diodorus of Sicily, there was one which gave leave to women to put away their husbands and to marry whom they liked. An old man, thus deserted by a young wife, proposed and carried an amendment of the import that whichever party, husband or wife, initiated the divorce, the said party should be forbidden to marry one younger than the former partner, whereupon the woman returned to his bed and board again. We put no great faith in the story, much less in the ascription of the law to Charondas. We give it only as a specimen of the legislation that was going on, wherever free

Greeks could govern themselves, and which, although in general starting from the same conceptions of marriage, and making divorce exceedingly easy, yet without doubt would exhibit, if it had been preserved, various peculiarities in different parts of the Greek world.

It is probable that after the Macedonian conquest these differences of legislation, where Greek States were autonomous—and that they were so to some extent even in Roman times is well known—were obliterated, and that a general average conception of the family relations, having almost nothing of morality in it, pervaded the whole race. The Greeks still adhered to monogamy, still allowed concubinage with scarcely a frown, still granted almost unlimited freedom to the separation of man and woman.

It is pleasant in this state of public feeling to know that a few voices were lifted up in favor of a somewhat better practice. The testimony of Plato in his Laws is worthy of mention.* He would take away from the parties interested the license of separation, and place divorce under the control of State authorities. If, says he, through infelicity of character a man and his wife cannot

* The principal authorities besides passages of authors, and especially of Demosthenes in his private orations, are the writers on Attic law, especially Meyer and Schömann's Attische Process, page 408, onward; Platner's Process, part 2, page 245; and the writers on archæology, especially K. F. Hermann.

agree together, let the case be put into the hands of ten impartial guardians of the law, and ten of those women to whom the matter of marriages is committed. Let them reconcile the parties if they can; and if not let them act according to their best ability in providing them with new spouses. If the philosopher means that the new yokes are to be laid on by force, it would most probably act as a restraint on divorce, and check the desire of separation, but whether it would do any other good might be reasonably doubted. This is about as far as the gospel of beauty could go. Plato's own view of marriage is certainly far from being the most elevated one, as his Republic testifies. It needed a gospel of holiness to put the Greek mind on a better track in regard to marriage and divorce.*

DIVORCE AMONG THE ROMANS.

The Romans had more of the moral and the religious in their character than the Greeks, as is manifest from that strong sense of justice and love of established form which pervades their law, and from that ancient fear and superstitious worship of the gods which ran down in the end into the merest formality. Their early institutions, more than those of any western nation, partake of patriarchal life. The closeness of the family tie,

* Leges xi., p. 930, A.

the septs or *gentes* of the patricians, and the vast powers of the *housemaster* over wife, children, and slaves, which it took ages to undermine, all point in that direction; and their peculiar veneration for ancient form in all things is of the same source. In fact so essential is the early constitution of the household to the Roman State, that State life, as it first shows itself, may be said to have grown directly out of family life.

Roman marriage in its earliest forms was for the wife a passing out of her natural family, where she was under the absolute control of its head, into the family of her husband, whose control was nearly the same as that of her father or grandfather. She was now said to be in his *hand*, and the marital power was known by the name of *manus*. There were three forms known to early Roman times by which the *manus* was acquired by the husband. Of these, without entering into the province of Roman archæology, it seems necessary to say a word for the better comprehension of the subject. The oldest of these, *confarreation*, which was exclusively patrician, was celebrated with special formalities by public priests in some sacred place before witnesses, and the *manus* was acquired by the same act by which the marriage was solemnized. This may be called *religious marriage*. The two others arose, as it seems, in plebeian life. Of these, *usus* was probably the earlier, a kind of prescription, in which, when the bride, after the regular betrothal and nuptials, had cohabited with her husband for a year without an absence of three successive nights, the *manus* or marital power was fully secured. Here the marriage and the *manus* originated in two acts widely separated in point of time. The remaining form of originally plebeian origin—*co-emption*—was a kind of fictitious sale, much like that used in adoption and emancipation, and here two contemporaneous acts give legal existence to the *manus* and the marriage. These may be called forms of *civil marriage*. This last form had become obsolete before Gaius wrote his institutions in the second century of our era. The two others were in a state of decay under the earlier Roman emperors.

At an early date, we have no means of knowing when, but long before Cicero's time, and before the age of the comic poets, a free kind of marriage without the *manus* came into vogue. It was preceded by betrothal and nuptials with religious ceremony. The connection was legitimate, jural, and respectable. In fact, had it not been so, there would at length have been no marriage at all, for this became in the end the universal form among the Romans. Its essence consisted chiefly in these particulars; that the union between the woman and her natural family was not sundered, and that the husband acquired no *manus* and no rights over any part of her property except the *dower*. The motive which gave rise to this kind of marriage may have been the unwillingness of the woman's father to lose control over her and her property in favor of one who was suspected or imperfectly known. It is one, and perhaps the earliest, of a series of innovations, by which patriarchal, patrician Rome surrendered its ancient iron habits, under the humanizing and loosening influences that followed in the track of civilization and of empire.

The two kinds of Roman marriage differ greatly when the power of dissolving the marriage union is considered. In the forms by which the *manus* was acquired the wife had no rights over herself or next to none, while the husband could dismiss her from his house at his pleasure. In the free form of marriage, the husband and the person who exercised the paternal power over the married woman, or she herself, if she was *sui juris*, had concurrent right to effect the separation of the parties. Of such authority exercised by the wife's father the comic poets of Rome furnish us with instances, but in process of time, if he took this step where there was an harmonious union and perhaps a family of children, the husband had a legal remedy against him.

The husband himself, moreover, was to some extent controlled by a very remarkable Roman institution, which derived its sanction from old custom rather than from positive law,—a family court, consisting of blood-relations of both parties, together with the husband himself. Such a court was also assembled to try great crimes of children, and yet there was not the same necessity for assembling it, according to Roman feeling, as where a guilty wife was to be brought to trial. And on the other hand, where a husband had neglected to call such a court before inflicting penalty on his wife, his neglect was not punishable as a wrong, but rather as an offense against good manners. It is recorded of one Lucius Antonius (about the year of the city, 440), that he was removed from the Senate by the censors for having repudiated his wife without taking council of friends, but the same stigma might have been put upon him for expensiveness, or other conduct not exactly illegal. In the freer kind of marriage, as the husband acquired no power over his wife's person, the head of her natural family must have called such a court, if any were assembled.

Divorce, according to a tradition preserved by Dionysius, was regulated by law from the time of Romulus onward. He says that it could take place for violations of the law of chastity and for drinking wine,—sentence of the husband and the relations being necessary for its validity. Plutarch's statement is that the wife could not separate herself from her husband, but that the husband could repudiate his wife for three crimes—poisoning the children, making false keys, and adultery. Wine-bibbing on the part of the wife we know from other sources to have been a grave offense. He adds that a man putting away his wife on other grounds forfeited his property, half of which was to be consecrated to Ceres, and half to go to the injured partner.* But these traditions can be of no historical value. They only show that divorce in the olden times was in some way restricted, and that family courts were of great antiquity.

A more reliable, yet no doubt confused, tradition declares the first divorce at Rome to have occurred about the year 520 of the city—that is eighty years after the divorce of Lucius Antonius already mentioned—and under the following circumstances: Carvilius Ruga is said to have greatly loved his wife who was barren, but inasmuch as the regular question of the Censor, at the time of the *census*, required him to declare, on oath, that he had, or would have, a wife *liberorum quærendorum gratia*, under pretense of avoiding a false oath, he terminated the marriage state by repudiation.† It is impossible to believe that no divorce occurred at Rome for more than five hundred years from its foundation, and yet there is no good reason for

* Dion. Hal., ii., 25; Plut., Romulus, § 22. Plutarch adds, that a man who sold his wife, in which plebeian marriage forms may have been practiced, was devoted to the infernal gods.

† It is preserved by A. Gell., iv., 3, xvii., 21; 13 Valer. Max., ii., 1, and by other writers. For explanation of it we refer to Rein's Röm. Privatrecht, p. 208, and to an essay in Savigny's vermischt. Schrift, vol. i., No. 4. He violated public feeling and his conscientious scruples were a mere pretext.

rejecting the story altogether. Various have been the attempts to explain it or to reconcile it with the probable state of facts. It may have been the first divorce in which a family court was not called, or the first in which no fault on the part of the wife could be alleged, and in which, without her consent, the husband terminated the union.

This was just before the second Punic war. The victories over Carthage, the extension of the Roman empire in Greece and the East, conspired with internal political changes and with the decline of religious fear, to hasten on a corruption of manners and of morals, a luxury and an avarice greater perhaps than any other nation ever reached. Rome was built on family discipline, on economy, thrift, and order, rather then on domestic affection. The Roman matron, austere by the discipline of life, was not much loved,—she was the house mistress simply. As soon as the old rigor of family life passed away, every thing in morals fell, and marriage was poisoned at its foundation. At the same time the increasing prevalence of the free form of marriage put it into the power of the wife's nearest relations to dissolve the union for her, and her own position became increasingly independent. Thus a step which only the husband could take under the old forms attended with the *manus*, could now be taken almost as freely by the wife; and a step which, in the older forms, needed a solemn formality in order to be valid, could now be taken with almost no formalities at all.* Add to this that the dower brought by the wife became almost an essential part of marriage, and avarice added its weight to the various other motives for divorce, if the chance of a better dower were offered. The dissolution of morals began with the upper classes at Rome, but the contagion could not help reaching the lower parts of society, the needy, shiftless freeman, the supple freedman, and the profligate foreigner, who made up a large part of the free population of Rome.

Toward the end of the Republic, then, things had reached this pass in regard to divorce:—that public opinion had ceased to frown upon it, that it could be initiated by husband or wife with almost equal freedom, that there was a ready consent of both parties to the separation in the prospect of marrying again, and that this facility of divorce was open to all classes who could contract lawful marriage. It might be supposed that the crime of adultery would be diminished by the power thus furnished of entering into a new marriage

* In the *confarreatio* or religious marriage of the patricians, a form called *diffarreatio*—that is, separation with the ceremony of offering the cake of spelt, as *confarreatio* denoted union with the same ceremony—dissolved the marriage tie. In both *coemptio* and *usus*, it is probable, a form called *remancipatio*, another fictitious sale, set the wife free from her husband. In marriage without the *manus* no form was necessary, and this kind of marriage at the fall of the Republic had superseded the others almost entirely.

with an object of guilty attachment. But adultery too went along with divorce. They were both indications of a horrible corruption, and neither of them was a vent-hole large enough to let off alone the inward foul stench of family life. And if proof were wanted of this we need only refer to the legislation of Augustus, and to the continual allusions made to adultery by the poets of the imperial times, such as Juvenal and Martial.

A few particulars, however, illustrating the sunken condition of the Roman lady toward the end of the Republic, and the small degree of sanctity which the marriage tie had now come to have, will perhaps make more impression than the most emphatic general statements. Already, before the last age of the republic, there was a foreshadowing of a decline of family morals in the expensiveness and in the crimes of married women. It was not enough that the Censor could interfere by his almost unrestrained power as a conservator of public morals; sumptuary laws also, broken and disregarded to be re-enacted with new provisions, show what was felt to be an evil of family life. At an early time also poisoning of a husband by a wife is noticed by the Roman historians. The case mentioned by Livy, as occurring in the year 423 of the city (B. C. 331) wears the look of an incredible prodigy. A number of the principal men having died without known cause, a maid gave information to one of the ædiles that some of the leading matrons had prepared and administered poisonous drinks. The case was looked into by order of the Senate, twenty were put to death at first, being compelled to take their own potions, and as many as one hundred and seventy were condemned afterward (Livy, viii., 18). Again about the year 572 (B. C. 182) the wife of a consul was convicted by many witnesses of having poisoned her husband; and a little later, just before the third Punic war, two of the first ladies of Rome, being convicted of the same crime by a court of relatives, were put to death.*

Nor ought we to overlook that frightful development of mingled superstition and lust, the affair of the Bacchanals, which so much alarmed the Senate, on account of its political as well as its moral aspects in the year of the city 568 (B. C. 186), and which in the very circumstances of its detection gives us a dark picture of family life, and discloses to us, as it were before the time, the corruption of Roman morals. It is to the year prior to that which brought these things to light, that Livy assigns the introduction of foreign luxuries through the soldiery who had served in Asia;—the costly garments and furniture, the singing women and sumptuous feasts, the cook, "vilest of slaves in the view of the forefathers," but now regarded as an artist. Yet, adds he, what was then witnessed was but the seeds of a luxury that was to come. The corruption that grew from the time of Sulla to that of Catiline, which

* Livy, xl., 37, and Epit. xlviii.

Clodius helped to increase, at the acme of which that "strong-minded" woman, Fulvia, and then such a person as Julia, an emperor's daughter, flourished, is acknowledged and painted in glaring col ors by the Roman historians. They are more apt, however, to dwell on avarice, lust of power, and luxury as the groundwork of the evil, not making enough of the decay of religion and the family, and less aware of the poisonous influence of slavery. The satirist Juvenal speaks thus of the sources of the corruption:

> Nullum crimen abest facinusque libidinis, ex quo
> Paupertas Romana perit.

And again,

> Prima peregrinos obscœna pecunia mores
> Intulit, et turpi fregerunt secula luxu
> Divitiæ molles.

But Horace goes more to the roots of things, when he says

> Fecunda culpæ secula nuptias
> Primum inquinavere et genus et domos.
> Hoc fonte derivata clades
> In patriam populumque fluxit.

We know Rome best during the last age of the republic, or at least biography and anecdote preserve more details of the private life of that period. Let us look at a few of these details which touch on divorce and domestic morals.

First we notice cases in which a slight impropriety on the part of the woman furnished ground for divorce. Here the ancient severity and a weakening of the family tie mingled their influences in one. A Sulpicius Gallus put away his wife because she had gone abroad with her head uncovered. An Antistius Vetus did the same, because his wife was seen by him talking in public with a freedwoman of the common sort; and a Sempronius Sophus, because his wife went to the spectacle without his knowledge. These may have been early cases: then, as morals fell and divorce grew common, mere dislike, or a fancy for some one else, caused men and women to desert their partners with a very summary notice, such as *tuas res tibi habeto.* An early instance of this occurs in the case of Æmilius Paullus, who put away Papiria, the mother of Scipio Africanus the younger, without giving any reasons for the step. Another striking instance is mentioned by a correspondent of Cicero, that of Paulla Valeria, the sister of Triarius, who divorced herself from her husband on the day that he was to return from his province, for the purpose of marrying Decimus Brutus. Innumerable must have been the cases of this kind. As numberless were divorces on the ground of adultery, provoked very frequently, where the wife committed the crime, by the intolerable dissoluteness and disregard of the husband. Only the fear of having to pay back the *dower* seems now to have restrained divorce, and this was often counteracted, as has been remarked, by a greater advantage in prospect.

The lives of many of the most eminent Romans show how loose was the marriage tie, or how great the crimes of one of the parties.

L. Lucullus, the conqueror of Mithridates, repudiated two wives on account of their infidelity—Claudia, daughter of a consul, and then Servilia, half-sister of Cato the younger. Her sister, another Servilia, the mother of Brutus, Cæsar's murderer, was a favorite mistress of Julius Cæsar. Cæsar was married four times:—his first wife, Cossutia, he divorced in his youth, to marry the daughter of the infamous Cinna; his third wife, Pompeia, he divorced on suspicion of an intrigue between her and Clodius, who came by stealth into her husband's house, in female attire, at the celebration of the mysteries of the Bona Dea. Cæsar himself was notorious for his impurity and libertinage, so that his soldiers scoffed about it in a triumphal procession. Pompey, a less immoral but much meaner man, repudiated his first wife, Antistia, to please the dictator Sulla, and his third, Mucia, on account of her profligacy. What shall we say of Cicero, one of the best of the Romans, who dismissed Terentia without crime, after a long marriage, to unite himself with a rich young lady, Publilia, in the hope of paying his debts out of her property. This connection, also, proved unfortunate, and was dissolved in about a year. Nor was his daughter Tullia less happy in her matrimonial affairs. Her first husband dying, she married a second, from whom ere long she divorced herself, and then became the wife of a most profligate man, Dolabella, who divorced his wife Fabia, it is said, to marry her. Cato the younger was married twice, and the second wife was worthy of him, but the first, Atilia, he divorced for adultery, after she had borne him two children. To these specimens, drawn from the families of the leading men at Rome, a rich collection might be added. If we now go down a little to Augustus, who forced the husband of Livia to repudiate her for his benefit, and took her to wife three months before the birth of a child by her first husband, or to his minister Mæcenas, who was as scandalous in his life as he was elegant in his taste, or to the profligate life of Julia, the emperor's daughter, and of so many other ladies of the house of the Cæsars, we shall find that family life grew worse instead of better, as the republic fell. There were indeed efforts made to effect a reform. Augustus, profligate himself, endeavored to alter morals by legislation—first in the year 727 (B. C. 27), then in 736 (B. C. 18), by several laws, among which the *lex Julia de adulteriis et de pudicitia* may be mentioned, and finally in 762 (A. D. 9), by the *lex Papia Poppæa.* Of these laws, so far as they related to divorce, we shall say at present but a word, although they form an epoch in the Roman legislation concerning the family relations. Divorce was now subjected to certain formalities, being invalid if not declared before seven grown-up Roman men and a freedman of the divorcing party. The man whose wife was caught in adultery or found guilty of it was obliged to put her away, on penalty of being held privy to the crime, and it was made incumbent on him to prosecute in such a case within sixty days, after which any other person might act as her accuser. A woman convicted of this crime was punished with relegation and a loss of a certain portion of her dower and of her goods. A freedwoman marrying her patron could not take out a divorce without his consent. This legislation also settled more fully and minutely a principle already acted upon, that in suits concerning dower after divorce the fault of the wife subjected her to a detention of a portion of the dower. This in the practice of Roman law seems to have been a most important matter, but its details do not belong here.

Augustus, and even that frightful wretch Tiberius, acted as legislators in the department of family morals. But morals grew worse and worse. He who is shocked by the developments of family life in the oration for Cluentius, or by such a character as Aurelia Orestilla, who, being reluctant to marry Cataline on account of a grown-up son, consummated the union when the son was made way with,—he who is shocked by these earlier acts of wickedness will be more shocked by what Suetonius and that tragic historian Tacitus have to tell of life under the emperors. It was then that Seneca, a man better skilled in writing than in acting morally, could say that no woman was now ashamed of divorce, since certain illustrious and noble ladies counted their years not by the number of consuls but of husbands. The moral disease had reached the vitals, and was incurable. As Rome rose to her greatness by severity of family life, so she fell into ruins by laxity just at that point.

Rome is a most interesting study for us Americans, because her vices, greed for gold, prodigality, a coarse material civilization, corruption in the family, as manifested by connubial unfaithfulness and by divorce, are increasing among us. We have got rid of one of her curses, slavery, and that is a great ground of hope for the future. But whether we are to be a thoroughly Christian nation, or to decay and lose our present political forms, depends upon our ability to keep family life pure and simple.*

* For divorce among the Romans, Wächter's work on that subject (Stuttgart, 1822), Rein's Privatrecht (Leipzig, 1836), Bekker-Marquardt's Roman Antiquities, part v. (Leipzig, 1861), and Rosbach's Roman Marriage, deserve, among many others, especial mention.

CHAPTER II.

DOCTRINE OF DIVORCE IN THE NEW TESTAMENT.

NOTHING places in a more striking light the sway of Christ over the mind of the Christian world than the fact that a few hints of his have been enough to turn the opinions and the practice of men into a new channel. This is illustrated by what he says of divorce; in giving commands concerning which he passes outside of his ordinary line of teaching, and enters into the region of positive external morality, instead of confining his precepts to the regulation of the thoughts and the affections. What he says on this subject is small in compass, it is a moral rule, and not a law for a state, it leaves more than one problem to be solved, and yet it has to a great extent controlled Christian law in an important branch of private relations, it has directed the discipline of the Church, it has helped to purify the family, and thus has aided the spread of the Gospel. It was, moreover, eminently needed at the time when it was made known. We hope to have shown, in our first chapter, that the great looseness and corruption, in the marriage relations, of the three nations to whom the world owes most of its progress, called for a reform, that there was need that a higher idea of marriage, a deeper sense of its sanctity should be placed among men, and a community be formed where the practice should be consonant with the idea. This has been done by Christ through his church; and they who receive him as the Lord from heaven, when they reflect that he is abstinent and reserved on most points of external morality, will admire the wisdom which led him to be outspoken on this. We propose, in the present chapter, to examine his words relating to divorce which are on record, and then to proceed to a consideration of the Apostle Paul's precepts on the same subject.

The passages in the Gospels which bear on the subject of divorce are contained in Matthew v. 31, 32; xix. 3–9; Mark x. 2–12; and Luke xvi. 18. The second and third of these passages were evidently uttered on the same occasion in reply to tempting questions put by Pharisees, and with some differences of importance they have the same strain of thought. The passage in Luke is found in company with verses, between which the connection of thought is hard to be traced, in an address or reply to the sneers of covetous Pharisees. When we compare this passage with that in the Sermon on the Mount, the disjointed thoughts in Luke have a light thrown upon them, and appear to be fragments of the same discourse. Without the place in Matthew we could find no law of association in Luke, or at most could only guess at one. But with the help of the first gospel, verse 17 of Luke, "and it is easier for heaven and earth to pass than one tittle of the law to fail," occurring as it does in Matthew, chap. v., and being an essential part of that wonderful sermon, is seen to have a vital union with verse 18, which treats of divorce. Either then Luke gives us detached parts of the sermon, or Christ repeated his instructions in similar forms on different occasions, in the one case delivering them to the people, in the other to the Pharisees. Which of these harmonizing theories is to be chosen it is not our business here to decide. We assume that our Lord expressed himself at least twice on the subject of divorce, and not once only, for we assume that there was a connected discourse on the mount, and that the words in Matthew, v. 31, 32, fit too well into that discourse not to have belonged to it from the first.

The principal differences between these places of the gospels are the following:—1. Matthew in both his passages adds a condition under which divorce is permissible,—"except on the ground of fornication," "but for fornication,"—while Mark and Luke express a prohibition of divorce which is altogether absolute. It is easy to say with Meyer, that the condition, being understood of course, did not require to be expressed. But we ought to notice that St. Paul also, when he refers to our Lord's teaching, inserts no condition whatever. We have, then, three witnesses to the absence of the condition against one for it, and the conjecture is not altogether improbable that it was added for the sake of greater clearness in Matthew, rather than omitted out of brevity by the others as being understood of itself.* Upon the meaning of *πορνεία* and the condition itself, we shall speak hereafter.

2. Mark has the important addition, "if a woman shall put away her husband and be married to another she committeth adultery." Now as by Jewish law a woman had no power whatever to put away her husband, this certainly looks like an addition to the original words of Christ, intended for the relations of believers in the heathen countries, where wives could procure divorce as well as husbands. But here again Paul supports Mark in 1 Cor. vii. 10: "unto the married I command, yet not I but the Lord, let not the wife be separated from her husband." What if by the law of Moses the wife could not be active in a case of divorce, we know that this occurred in the family of Herod, and it is likely that Greek or Roman custom may

* As in Romans, vii. 2, 3, where the apostle says broadly, "to the living husband," "while the husband is living," although the law allowed the wife, when put away, to marry another during the first husband's life-time.

already have begun to creep into Palestine; at least the license of divorce allowed by the rulers of the world could not have escaped the knowledge of our Lord. Why is it incredible then that he should have contemplated the case of a woman putting away her husband?

3. In Matthew xix. our Lord says every thing in the presence of the Pharisees. In Mark x. he gives out the principle of the indissolubility of marriage, and then in the house expounds the matter further to his disciples. Some critics see a mistake or inaccuracy here. If there were any, it must be laid at Matthew's door, for the words of Mark, "and in the house the disciples asked him again of this matter," give proof of fresh clear recollection. But is there any thing forced here in the supposition that our Lord went over again to his disciples with what he had said just before, so that there was no need on the part of either evangelist to give an account of the whole conversation. In Matthew the disciples felt perplexed by what he had said, and put him further questions. They would not readily do this before the carping Pharisees, and so Mark's statement that the subject was continued in the house is justified, and his account of what was said in the house rendered at least probable.

Having thus discussed the form in which our Lord's words appear, let us now look at their purpose and their import. Here the *first* thing to be noticed is that our Lord acts the part not of a civil legislator, but of a supreme moral teacher. He does not establish a law concerning divorce, but declares that the existing code permits certain things which must be condemned as wrong, as violating high ethical rules acknowledged by the law itself. Every moral teacher, not to say every moral man, must take the same position in regard to the laws of his country. These may, in fact they must, fail to forbid many things which sound morality condemns. The law is an external, general, coarse, imperfect rule, commanding often what the ethical code requires and as frequently permitting what that code prohibits. If there were any permissions of the Jewish law which ran counter to true righteousness, if it afforded any facilities for transgression which ought to be cut off, it was the business of Christ to notice them and to animadvert against them. Herein he differs in no respect from any other moral teacher. Nor are these verses touching divorce peculiar in this respect. When he cites the *lex talionis* of the Old Testament, "an eye for an eye, and a tooth for a tooth," he tells his hearers that justice as expressed in the law might permit this to be done, but there was something higher then justice; "resist not evil" was a better law of life, a law necessary for any one who would be his disciple.

Now it might happen, as it has happened, that some of these rules propounded by our Lord would reform and transform legislation. Such, owing to the fact that marriage has most important civil, moral, and religious relations, would inevitably be the result of the utterances concerning divorce. Still they are not properly legislation, but they are principles which in lands under a Christian faith must leaven all legislation.

Secondly, the tone our Lord uses, and the ground on which he puts his restrictions of divorce, show at once a remarkable depth of thought and the consciousness of an authority such as pertains to a divine messenger. The man who beyond all others was nourished by the scriptures and reverenced the scriptures, criticises a provision of the Mosaic law, and taxes it with imperfection. In so doing he boldly lays down a principle of the utmost importance and of far-reaching consequences, —that the Mosaic economy, although given by God, was rudimentary, transitory, and accommodated to the state of a nation not yet capable of the highest kind of civil polity. There is in his words even the germ of an abolition of the old economy, the beginning of a judgment pronounced against the old rites, in short against the old religion in its external forms; for if divorce was permitted on account of the hardness of the people's hearts, why might not the forms of the ceremonial law be accommodated to an early stage of their progress and be unsuitable for a more advanced stage. Thus our Lord, without seeming to do so, drove that entering wedge into the law, which

Paul and his school drove further, until all men saw that it was done away in Christ.

Nor is the reason which our Lord gives for his new morality, in the matter of divorce, less remarkable. The freedom allowed by the law, he says, was inconsistent with the true primeval conception of marriage. Law, a patchwork of expedients, needs not to conform to the true conception of human relations,—that is to say, there are times, there is a state of feeling, a "hardness of hearts," which stand in the way of perfect legislation, although the nearer the law approaches to that standard, the greater the proof and the greater the security of the genuine culture of the people. But morality must conform to the true idea, and it is the highest merit of a moral teacher, if he has the idea bright in his own mind and is able to set it forth to his fellow-men. Christ had this idea. He who never drew from experience any judgments concerning the human relations of which he here speaks, whose vocation was too high for the entanglements of family life,—this man corrects the judgments of men by a reference to the essential nature of marriage; it is the state of life in which two have become one flesh, it is a state founded by God at the first creation of man, it is therefore a union made by divine authority which human authority may not sever.

Before proceeding to the special rules which our Lord lays down, we remark that he does not side with either of the two schools which then divided opinion among the Jews on the subject of divorce. The doctrines of Hillel* of course he utterly discards, but he does not give his adhesion to those of Shammai any more than in the conversation with the Samaritan woman he pronounces altogether for the Jews against her nation. In fact it is altogether probable that his rule is far stricter than that of the school of Shammai, and he shows no interest in the explanation of Deut. xxiv. 1–5, about which the Rabbis wrangled. His interest is moral, his views are general and human, not Jewish and Mosaical, while his line of thought must have surprised the tithers of mint, anise, and cummin.

What then does he lay down? His rules may be all comprised in the following propositions:

First, that the man who in conformity with the permission or sufferance of the law puts away his wife by a bill of divorcement,—"saving for the cause of fornication"—and marries another commits adultery, or, as Mark has it, commits adultery "against her," or to her injury.

Second, that the man who thus puts away his wife causes her to commit adultery, that is, by placing it within her power to marry whom she pleases leads her to form an adulterous connection, inasmuch as she is still his wife in the eye of God. Matthew alone preserves this declaration.

* See Chapter I., page 15.

Third, that the man who marries her who has thus been put away commits adultery. This rule is contained in both places of Matthew, and in Luke, but not in Mark.

Fourth, that the woman who puts away her husband and is married to another commits adultery. As we have already had occasion to say, Mark alone has recorded this declaration, but is sustained by the Apostle Paul.

The general principle, serving as the groundwork of all these declarations, is, that legal divorce does not in the view of God and according to the correct rule of morals authorize either husband or wife thus separated to marry again, with the single exception that when the divorce occurs on account of a sexual crime the innocent party may without guilt contract a second marriage.

In the application of these precepts for the guidance of the church of Christ, we assume for the present that whatever is said only of the husband may be said, *ceteris paribus*, of the wife also. Had the case of a woman divorcing herself from her husband never been put on record by Mark, the reason of the rule would have applied equally to her, and the fact that Jewish law never gave the woman the power to commence proceedings in a divorce would have sufficiently accounted for all silence respecting cases of that description. This case is plain enough, but there are questions of some importance and of some difficulty growing out of our Saviour's words which need to be considered.

We notice in the first place the fact that nothing is said of the remarriage of a party—a woman for instance—divorced on account of her crime. It has been gravely argued in our country and our time, that inasmuch as the married pair are no longer one flesh after crime, the guilty one is free to marry again, yes, even to marry the tempter or seducer, and that this is no violation of the law of Christ. We admit that Christ observes silence on this point. He could not say that such a guilty author of a divorce committed adultery by marrying again, for she is now free from her husband. But it would have been idle to refer to such a case, for in the first place it had nothing to do with the immediate point on which Christ expresses an opinion, and in the second place such a person would have been punishable by Jewish law with death. To claim for an adulterer and an adulteress the protection of law in a Christian state, so that, when free through their crime from former obligations, they may legally perpetuate a union begun in sin, is truly to put a premium on adultery. A Herod on that plan, after sinning with his brother's wife, would need only to wait for legal separation to convert incest into legitimate wedlock.

Another question of importance relates to the meaning of *πορνεία* in the two passages of Matthew. Is it synonymous with *μοιχεία* or does it embrace unchaste acts not going to that length? Can it include acts committed before marriage, or must it be confined to sins which violate the marriage covenant? Interpreters might be named who have given latitude to the word in one or the other of these respects. In regard to the question of time, it is enough to say that our Saviour's whole strain of remark assumes that the parties have become one flesh, and that one of them by the violence of crime has been torn away from the other. He does not go back of the commencement of marriage to inquire what previous crimes, frauds, deficiencies, or closeness of relationship made the union illegitimate *ab initio.* That he leaves to the civil law. He is not giving a lecture on marriage or making canons for church discipline; he is merely answering a question in regard to the termination of a marriage already existing. How then can we conceive him to have referred in his precepts to an antenuptial condition of things. To this, which is entirely conclusive, we might add a consideration which is only corroborative and has no independent force of its own, that in corrupt states of society a most alarming license would be given to divorce by making such a precept embrace a whole life-time, especially if the rule were applied alike to both sexes.

The word then relates to what has transpired *since* marriage. We add that it must refer to some *outward* act. It can not in its proper sense denote a mere quality, and, if ever used with a breadth of meaning to embrace sensual lust, it must be in the company of words which make its sense clear, like "in his heart," Matthew v. 28. It must intend a positive outward act which all would understand to be a violation of the obligations of marriage, a departure in essentials from its idea; for so we can best account for the omission of the condition in Mark, Luke, and St. Paul's writings, and for its appearance in Matthew alone. It must point to crime wrought by one of the married pair with a third person, not to wanton conduct in which the married pair unite, which might be called impurity, or lewdness, but never *πορνεία* in any proper sense. We have then, in assigning it a meaning, to choose between the narrowest sense, in which it is strictly synonymous with adultery, or a broader sense, including as well crimes more grave and bestial than adultery, as acts of attempted but interrupted crime. It seems hardly worth our while to decide whether the narrower or wider sense ought to prevail. Many of the best interpreters regard the word as equivalent to the more specific *μοιχεία*, and we are willing to accede to their opinion.*

* Origen seems to understand it thus, Tom. 14 of his comment. on Matthew (iii. 322, 323, ed. Lommatsch). So Greg. Naz. says (Or. 37), that Christ allows separation only from the *πόρνη*, because she *νοθεύει τὸ γένος*. Basil in his 21st canon cited by Suicer, voce *πόρνος* used that word in the same way, and Balsamon re-

But why should an exception like that in the two passages of Matthew be made, if πορνεία is the same as adultery, when the latter crime was punishable with death and thus divorce would seem to be superfluous. A conjectural answer might be drawn from the altered circumstances of the Jews in their later times, when intercourse with the more polished heathen, in whose eyes sexual crimes were not very heinous, tended to relax the strictness with which the law was enforced, and when the right of capital punishment was taken away from their courts by the Romans. But a better solution of the difficulty lies in this, that the husband was not bound, so far as appears, to denounce his guilty wife, but that it was the business of the local police to bring crimes before the local courts—the elders or presbytery of the commune—for their examination and sentence. Thus the husband, even in such cases, might give the ordinary bill of divorcement, leaving it to common fame to bring the matter before the po-

marks that he calls the adulterer a πόρνος. Euthymius in his commentary on Matthew v. 32, explains the one word by the other. All the most recent commentators of highest credit do the same. For opinions allowing a wider sense to the word, Tholuck (Bergpred., ed. 3, p. 229), who himself adheres to the sense which is here defended, and Alford in his note on Matthew v. 32, may be consulted. We may add that in Hosea ii. 3, where it is said of the wife whom he bought in symbol, "thou shalt not play the harlot," there is the same substitution of the more general for the more specific term.

lice magistrates.* This view of Jewish usage gives a better explanation of Jer. iii. 8, than that which we gave in the first chapter. God is there spoken of as putting adulterous Israel away, and as giving her a bill of divorce, and if our present explanation is the right one, there was no deviation in this from the usage in actual cases of adultery. The husband put away his wife, and on the magistrates devolved the duty of bringing her to justice. With this agrees what is said of Joseph, in Matthew i. 19. He was a just man, and therefore unwilling that the supposed crime of his betrothed should go unrebuked, and yet being reluctant to expose her, he made up his mind to put her away so as not to attract public notice. Justice was satisfied in his view, so far as he was concerned, when he abrogated the contract by a private separation.†

But there are frightful crimes against nature, odious even to the heathen: supposing these not to be included in the term *πορνεία* will they furnish no ground for divorce? All that needs to be said here seems to be that death is the penalty for such crimes by Jewish and many other laws, so that the separation would be inevitable; that our

* Comp. Saalschütz, chapters 4 and 5, on the judges and the Shoterim.

† The notion at one time pretty common, that *δίκαιος* here means *mild, clement*, is now nearly exploded. The betrothed was treated as a wife by the law. Deut. xxii. 23.

Lord had no occasion to speak of gross crimes of very rare occurrence about which there could be no difference of opinion; and that if both he and the Pharisees admitted these crimes to be more than adultery, his exception by right reason would include them.

There ought to be, however, some reason why *πορνεία*, the generic word, is here used instead of the more specific *μοιχεία*. That reason can hardly be the rhetorical one of avoiding the repetition of the same word. Nor can it well be what Tholuck suggests, in his commentary on the Sermon on the Mount, that the generic word gives more indication of the moral category of the offense. Still less is De Wette's solution satisfactory—"that *μοιχεία* is avoided because the verb *μοιχᾶσθαι* is afterward used in a wider sense." Perhaps the explanation may be found in the consideration that as the same offense could be called by the one name in relation to the husband, and by the other in relation to the paramour, the word was naturally suggested.

The one exception made by our Saviour excludes all others, unless it can be shown that they are embraced under the same reason to an equal or greater extent. Meyer and Tholuck therefore justly rebuke De Wette for his loose assertion that in allowing one actual ground of divorce our Lord allowed more than one. The exception, when the indissoluble nature of marriage is the starting point, is of strict interpretation, or else such as all, at the time when it was made, would admit without its being mentioned. And this remark brings us to the passages in the two other Evangelists, and in Paul where no exceptional case is stated. The reason for these unqualified statements of the sacred writers is not—as Meyer well observes—that Christ conceded somewhat at first to Jewish marriages contracted before his church was established,* but that the two Evangelists and the Apostle regard the exception as a matter of course, and pass it over in silence. This they might well do, if the exception related to so great a crime as adultery, which of itself actually caused the married pair to be no longer one flesh, which violated the idea of marriage.

There is nothing in these passages, nor in our Saviour's principle in regard to marriage, nor in other passages of the New Testament, that can fairly be regarded as forbidding the innocent party, against whom the crime of adultery has been committed, to contract a second marriage. This severe opinion arose in the early church. Augustin advocated it in his treatise *de conjugiis*

* A worthy Catholic scholar, Hug, throws this out, and it would help the absolute indissolubility of marriage according to the view of that church, but it would require us to believe that "except it be for fornication," in Matt. xix., is an interpolation. Of this, however, although the reading varies, there is no good evidence.

adulterinis, although in his retractations* this nobly honest man doubts whether he has cleared up the matter in that work. The opinion became current and passed into canonical law. The Council of Trent, in the seventh canon on matrimony, pronounces a curse on him who taxes the church with error for teaching "that he commits adultery who puts away an adulterous wife and marries another woman, and that the woman commits the same crime who puts away an adulterous husband and marries another man." But this canon, which rests on a view of marriage not entirely scriptural, receives no sanction from the New Testament. It is most clear that the words "except it be for fornication" (Matt. xix. 9) allow divorce in that particular case, and that in the divorce spoken of, liberty of remarriage is implied. The question is, what must the parties to the conversation have understood by putting away, as our Lord here uses the word. How could they have guessed that he meant separation *quoad torum* only, which was not known to the law? Is it not evident that they were compelled to give that sense to his words which divorce had in the law of Moses about which they were talking. The permission then to put away a wife in this one case involves a permission of remarriage to the innocent party.

After the same analogy the parallel crime of

* Lib. ii., chap. 57.

the husband separates the married pair to the same extent, and involves permission of remarriage to the innocent wife. This is generally conceded by those who do not hold with the Catholics that marriage cannot in the absolute sense be dissolved by crime. But a difficulty here arises. What sense shall we attach to the word adultery—the narrower Jewish sense, or the broader one, which the word now generally carries with it? Among the Jews the wife and the husband were not on an equality; the husband might commit whoredom with an unmarried woman without being an adulterer; the wife was an adulteress when she fell into similar transgression. What then would our Saviour have meant, had he uttered the words used by Mark (x. 12), "and if a woman put away her husband," with the qualification found in Matthew, "saving for the cause of fornication?" If πορνεία could mean any lewd conduct inconsistent with being one flesh, the case might be clear, but this is, to say the least, doubtful, and we have not been able to admit it. As far then as the use of words is concerned we cannot infer that our Lord gave the same liberty of remarriage to the wife thus injured as to the husband similarly wronged. But when we consider that he must have viewed the husband's crime with an unmarried woman as a great one, as an equal violation of the marriage covenant with the wife's, as an equal breach of the original law or declaration that "they twain shall be one flesh," which excludes all sexual impurity of both alike with any one else, we believe that he would have placed both partners on the same ground, and given liberty of remarriage in that one case to the wronged woman. And yet in the absence of any words from our Lord, we do not hold this opinion with the same confidence as we hold that the liberty of remarriage for the man, when the woman is the offender, is clearly to be gathered from our Lord's precepts.

But may it not be said with Augustin,* that the precept of Paul, "if she depart, let her remain unmarried," can only be reconciled with the words of our Lord, on the supposition that this departure had taken place on the ground of the adultery of her husband. She could then put him away or depart from him, but according to Christian law had no liberty of remarriage; and she might be reconciled to him so as to live with him again. The same would be true, *mutatis mutandis*, of the husband, and thus forgiveness for the highest matrimonial crime would be in accordance with the spirit of the gospel, but remarriage be opposite both to its genius and its positive rules. Or, to express the argument in a word, Christ allows putting away only on account of adultery. But Paul conceives of a separation of one member of the church from another who is a husband or wife.

* De adult. conj., near the beginning.

Therefore this separation must be on the ground of adultery. But the party leaving the other must remain unmarried. Therefore the man or woman separated from a guilty partner must remain unmarried.

The only way of meeting this argument is to deny that separation is understood by Christ and Paul in the same sense, and to take the ground that the case of adultery was not before the Apostle's mind. Christ was arguing with the Pharisees on such divorces as were attended with a license of marrying again, and denies that any such could take place except in one specific instance. It is in the highest degree improbable that he had in his mind separations *a mensa et toro.* Did Paul draw the rule tighter, and deny that remarriage was lawful even in that specific instance? Or did he not rather contemplate such separations of an informal sort, begun without even the idea of remarriage, as might have occurred within the Christian Church? To us it appears that he meant such separations by his word χωρισθῇ, and he says in effect, if separated let her not commit adultery by marrying again, which she would do if she had left her husband for a cause falling short of adultery.

We now pass on to that important passage in the first of Corinthians, where the Apostle Paul handles the subject of divorce. Two cases are here noticed, one for which the Lord had given commandment, where both the parties were Christian believers, and another which had not been provided for by the Saviour's authority, where one of the parties was an unbeliever. In regard to the first case, the Apostle must refer to the commandment contained in the extant words of Christ, or to some other of similar import. We have already observed that he coincides with Mark in speaking of a wife divorcing herself from her husband, and with both Mark and Luke in omitting the exception which Matthew twice inserts in his Gospel. How the exception came to be omitted we have tried to explain, and the explanation will derive additional weight from a similar omission in Rom. vii. 2, where, when it broadly said that the wife is bound by the law to her husband as long as he liveth, the Apostle puts out of sight the husband's freedom of divorcing the wife which the law itself concedes to him.

The commandment of Christ is limited, as we conceive, by the Apostle to the case where both partners in the marriage are believers, because only in such a case could it be regarded as the practical law of the household, whatever might be the law of the land, and in such a case its infraction would always fall under the jurisdiction of the church. In the other case one of the parties would feel bound to submit to a commandment to which the other attached no binding force. It may be that the Apostle regarded marriage to be as indissoluble in itself for partners of diverse faith, or even for two heathen, as for two Christian believers. The principle uttered by Christ of the "one flesh," he may have fully received as applicable to marriage in general, and yet there was need of discussing a second case, not because the principle here was different, but because it contained difficulties which needed to be considered by themselves. We must not impute to the Apostle the opinion that Christ's precept was not as broad as the reasons on which it was based, but the gospel in its spread met persons whose subjective state could not be controlled by the precept: there was need therefore of advice for those whom such persons affected by their conduct.

The Apostle's repetition of the Gospel precept, besides the prohibition there found, contains the decision of a case that may have existed at the very time in the Corinthian church. Let not the wife separate herself from her husband. But should she even have separated herself,—which seems to imply that instances of this kind had occurred and were known to the Apostle,—let her remain unmarried or be reconciled to her husband. Here the latter words imply that the separation was due not to any crime on the husband's part, but to dissensions between the married pair. And the Apostle allows the wife who has gone so far—such is the sense of *καὶ*—as even to withdraw from her husband and to live apart, the choice between remaining unmarried and returning, after an amicable settlement of the difficulties, to the former condition. Here the verb denoting separation is somewhat indefinite in its sense. It can denote simple withdrawal from the husband's house and society without any formal act by which remarriage would be legalized, or it can include the declaration of a purpose of divorce besides. We question whether it means so much as this, although it is used as the equivalent of ἀφίημι. For the Apostle says, "let her be reconciled," which seems to imply that mere peace between the parties and return to the husband was all that she had need of, as not having already taken the step of a legal separation. Yet, on the other hand, the expression "let her remain unmarried," implies the power of sooner or later contracting a *legal* marriage with another man. But whatever may be thought of this, it is obvious that the Apostle conceives of a state of things in which a woman, separated from her husband, and that, it may be, permanently, shall have no right, according to the Lord's commandment, of marriage with another man. In other words, we have here an actual separation *a mensa et toro* without a separation *a vinculo matrimonii*. This third state between absolute divorce and the full marriage union has then the sanction of the Apostle,—not of course as something desirable, but probably as a kind of barricade against divorce and a defense of the Saviour's commandment. It may be introduced therefore into the law of Christian lands.

From cases where both parties were Christian believers the Apostle passes on to a new kind of cases, doubtless frequent enough, for which Christ had not provided,—those in which one of the parties had received the Gospel, while the other still continued a heathen. In regard to all such cases the Apostle's words involve, without expressing fully, the principle that the believing party is not to initiate any steps which will terminate the marriage union, but must remain passive, while all active proceedings are expected to emanate from the other side. Thus should the unbelieving husband or wife be content to dwell with the Christian partner, the latter may not put the other away. This is the first case that is noticed, and it was doubtless of frequent occurrence. Here Paul meets a feeling to which the new faith itself might give rise. So great was the transition from the foul worship of impure divinities to the faith in Christ and in a God of holiness, that close connection with a heathen, however ignorantly or innocently begun, might seem unclean and unhallowed. To this he replies, without mentioning the feeling itself, that the heathen partner is hallowed by the believing one, that marriage and the marriage bed preserve their sanctity because one of the parties is a consecrated person. Otherwise the children would be unclean, whereas all admit that they are consecrated. Without stopping to discuss the Apostle's meaning here, it is enough if we say that he draws a broad line between a family where both parents are heathen and another where one is a Christian.

But the heathen, whose husband or wife had become a Christian convert, might be soured or alienated for that very reason, and might insist on terminating the union. The decision in this second case is expressed in these words: "But if the unbelieving depart let him depart." That is, if he separates himself from his Christian partner (or is in the act of separating himself, as some explain the tense), let him take his course unhindered. A believer has not by his profession been brought into slavery, is not under bondage in such cases, is not subjected to the obligation of keeping up the marriage relation and of preventing the disruption by active measures of his own. Such bondage would subject the believer to a state of warfare, but God's call to him, when he invites him into the Gospel, is in the form of peace. And moreover let not the believing party think that he ought to take on him this painful obligation in order to convert the heathen partner. For it is wholly uncertain whether by living with such a partner, when he is bent on separation, any such result will be attained.*

* The clause," but God has called us to peace, " is difficult. We have given the antithesis, represented by δέ, as pointing to

This is an important passage, as furnishing the authority, if there be any in the scripture, for divorce with remarriage on the ground of desertion. In rendering its meaning, as we have done, we have unavoidably shown a certain amount of bias on that question, because otherwise the connection of thought could not easily be presented. We will now return on our steps, glancing as briefly as possible at the leading interpretations of verses

a state of strife which Paul only hints at, for it seems to us to be implied in the word χωρίζεται. The expression "in peace," as the original is literally rendered, many make equivalent with *into peace*. Winer teaches us that Paul never uses ἐν as equivalent to εἰς, and explains it, "so as to be in peace," which is really admitting what he condemns. De Wette follows him. Harless and Meyer give the solution adopted in our paraphrase :—"God has called us in peace," *i. e.* God's call has come to us in the ethical form of peace. The words, "for what knowest thou—whether," were taken by nearly all the older commentators as implying the possibility that by living together with the heathen the Christian might save him or her. It would then be a dissuasive against separation. But logic will not bend to this rendering. We ought to have for it a different context. It would require τί δέ instead of τί γάρ, and the words scarcely admit of the version, "what do you know but that," or "how do you know that you will not." For an attempt of Tholuck to defend this way of understanding the interrogation, see his Bergpred, fourth edition, p. 252. Billroth, Rückert, Olshausen take it in the same way. It would strengthen our side to follow them, but this seems to us an inadmissible construction. Nor can verse 17 weigh in opposition. The condition in which the believer actually is, is one of desertion, not one of cohabitation with a husband or wife. Let him or her then remain in this state of desertion. The case is like that mentioned in verse 27.

15 and 16, then looking again at the connection, and finally, endeavoring to discover how the decisions of the Apostle can be brought into harmony with those of the Lord.

The greater part of the commentators, although by no means all, understand *οὐ δεδούλωται*, "is not under bondage," to deny the necessity of remaining unmarried, and infer from it the lawfulness of taking another husband or wife under the conditions specified by the Apostle. The Catholic Church, so strict in the matter of divorce, allows, and that in good part on the authority of this passage, both divorce and second marriage to a Christian separated from a heathen by the agency of the latter.* The prevailing view among the Protestants also has drawn a justification of divorce in cases of malicious desertion, whether the guilty party be a heathen or not, from this commandment of the Apostle. To some the bondage which the Apostle speaks of is that of remaining unmarried, or the alternative obligation of either remaining unmarried or being reconciled, so that the duty, where one of the parties is a heathen, is just the opposite of that prescribed in verse 11.

* We may have to revert to this again; at present it is enough to say that in passages of the Canon Law relating to this subject (Decret. Grat., ii. ,Caus. xxviii., Qu. 2, C. 2, and Decretals, iv., 19, de divortiis, Cap. 7), this text is cited as the authority. It should be added, however, that the opinion entertained in the ancient church concerning heathen marriage facilitated this allowance of remarriage where the parties had been heathen.

Others draw this right of remarriage as an inference from the scope of the passage, rather than rest it upon any particular expression. And the question may be asked with some force, why, if remarriage is not allowed, does the Apostle consider his commandment to be a new one. Is all the difference between the case in verse 11, and that in verse 15, that in the former the separated party must, and in the latter need not be reconciled to the other?

We will first look at the meaning of *οὐ δεδούλωται*. The verb has been compared by some with *δέδεται*, which in several places is made use of by the Apostle to denote the marriage bond (verses 27, 39; Rom. vii. 2). But in truth there is no connection between the two words. The one denotes an obligation merely, and the other a severe or painful obligation, an unfree subjection resembling that of slavery. It might without question be used on the proper occasion by an author who wished to express a harsh necessity of remaining unmarried. But the sense would lie not in the word, but in the context.

What then is the bondage which the context here points out? Meyer correctly answers that *οὐ δεδούλωται* does not deny the obligation to remain unmarried, as Grotius and others assert, but the necessity of continuing the married state; and so he remarks that the place gives no express answer to the question whether Paul concedes remarriage to the Christian party. Stanley on the passage remarks in the same strain, "that this is not so much a permission of separation as an assertion that, if on other grounds a separation has taken place, there is no obligation on the Christian partner to insist on a union." So, too, De Wette says, that "the positive side of this notion [*i. e.* of the notion of separation, viz.: remarriage] is certainly not brought forward by the Apostle, although it may be supplied by correct inference." Nor can we forbear to introduce a passage from Neander's commentary on Corinth. vii., for which our readers, we are sure, will thank us. "Protestant exegesis," he says, "has understood the Apostle to the effect that in such a case the Christian party would be authorized to enter into a new marriage. But this is not at all contained in the words. The Apostle simply means, that in things pertaining to religious conviction no one ought to be the slave of another, that the Christian partner cannot be forced to stay with the heathen, if the latter will not allow to the other the exercise of his religious convictions. In such circumstances a separation can be allowed, but of an allowance to contract another marriage there is not a word here said." And we close our citation of authorities with an extract from Tholuck's exposition of the Sermon on the Mount (p. 233, 3d ed.). "The words 'is not in bondage in such cases,'" says he, "have a direct reference only to living together,—and in verses 10, 11, χωρίζεσθαι is so used that with it reconciliation is thought of as still possible." And in the greatly altered 4th edition (p. 253), he expresses his opinion that "we can not find in the case of malicious desertion so called, which the Apostle adduces, a justification of remarriage."

With this view the Apostle's reasons agree, and show most clearly that whether he regarded remarriage in such cases as lawful or not, he can here have had no thought of it in his mind. The first of these reasons is that a compulsory cohabitation with an unbeliever, who disturbs his partner's peace, is not in accordance with the call of the Gospel. Here then reluctant living with a quarrelsome heathen, not any ultimate step such as remarriage, was in the Apostle's mind. The other reason is that the probability of converting such a heathen partner, so bent on separation, is not so great as to make remaining with him against his will a Christian duty. Here again nothing but dwelling in marriage relations with the heathen husband or wife is thought of. The Apostle's mind goes no further than that point, if we have fairly represented his train of thought, as we have tried to do in harmony with the opinions of the best modern interpreters. The Apostle then says simply this: "if the heathen is bent on separation, let him take his course. You are permitted to suffer this in order to preserve your peace. You are not bound to stay with him to secure his conversion, for this is an uncertain thing."

But, it maybe asked, why did the Apostle think it worth his while to give a decision in such cases, if the decision amounts only to a license of non-cohabitation, without granting the power of re-marriage? And does not the contrast of the cases in verses 11 and 15, show that the obligation required in the former verse—either to remain unmarried or to be reconciled—had no existence in the case of which the latter verse treats; that here, in fact, the believer is neither bound to remain unmarried nor to be reconciled to the infidel partner.

To the first of these fair objections we answer that a new case of duty, unknown among the members of a believing community gathered out of the Jews, came up where a church was gathered in gentile lands. Some there were who in their abhorrence of false gods and of idolatrous worship regarded an unconverted husband or wife as unclean; the contamination spread over the family relations, and a wife, for instance, looked with inward horror on a husband who sacrificed to Zeus or to Aphrodite, although he had been kind to her, and had no thought of separation. Others there were, whose heathen husbands, after interfering with their dearest rights and hopes, determined to separate from them, but who were morbidly conscientious lest by consenting to such separation they should hinder the conversion of the unbeliever. Was it not well worth the Apostle's while to tell persons so situated how they ought to act?

To the other objection we answer that it would be fair to infer that neither of the injunctions of the eleventh verse can be applied to the fifteenth, unless it could be shown, as we seem to ourselves to have shown, that the context proved the Apostle to have had no thought of remarriage in his mind.

To this we may add that there is a certain improbability, inherent in the case itself, that the Apostle would have given such a permission. The word *χωρίζεται* denotes any separation, whether attended with a formal statement of a purpose of divorce or not, in other words, it includes divorce and desertion. And the exemption from "bondage" began to exist as soon as the separation commenced. Now would the Apostle have given a license greater than any law of the loosest Christian State gives, when he must have been cognizant of instances in which husbands or wives, who had thus deserted their partners, had become converts within a few months, and were thus ready to be reconciled and to live in Christian wedlock? Would he not have added some qualification or advised some delay?

The view here presented brings the precepts of

our Lord and that of the Apostle into harmony, or at least shows that there is no necessary contradiction between them. The Christian wife or husband must accept as a fact what the unbelieving partner has done, but the marriage, so far as the Apostle lets his opinion be known, may still have been indissoluble, and the injured believer must remain in a state of desertion. All other ways of reconciliation, which proceed on the assumption that Paul permitted remarriage, are failures. Will any one say with De Wette in his Commentary, that both Christ and Paul permit remarriage, when the parties are separated in fact? But Christ, at the most, only allows it in cases of adultery, and if Paul allows it in other cases he enlarges the rule. To say that Christ, when he said, "except on account of fornication," only gave a sample of several exceptions which he regarded as valid, is to trifle with his words, and to leave the door open for any degree of laxness. Will it be said, as Meyer says, that Christ did not have mixed marriages in his mind, but only marriages within his church? We reply that he laid down a universal rule, and gave a reason of general application for his rule. If those Pharisees whom he addressed in Matthew, chap. xix., admitted the force of what he said, they would be bound to take it as the rule of their life, even if they could not admit his claims to be the Messiah. Why should the Christian partner in a marriage be released from obeying a command of his Lord, because the heathen would not submit to it? Or will it be said that Paul, and perhaps Christ, did not regard heathen marriage as marriage in the proper sense, but only as a kind of *contubernium*, to which the laws that govern Christian marriage were inapplicable. But the Apostle nowhere indicates that he holds any such opinion. Marriage with a heathen was, indeed, in his view a violation of Christian duty for one who was already a believer (2 Cor. vi. 14); but marriage contracted in a state of heathenism was a condition in which the heathen was called the husband or wife of the converted partner, in which the Christian was to remain if the heathen did not dissolve the union, in which the unbeliever himself partook of a kind of sanctity and the children were holy. To apply the rules of Ezra's time to the times of the kingdom of God, to require that the idolater must be separated from the believer in the near relations of life was not in accordance with Paul's strain of thinking. Marriage among the heathen, it is true, was far from conforming to the ideal presented to us in the earlier scriptures, where the man is conceived of as cleaving to his wife so closely as to bring her nearer to him than father or mother, and as becoming one flesh with her. But there was some purity left, there were examples of illustrious conjugal fidelity, and there were vices against marriage that "were not so much as named among the heathen." If on the whole it fell far short of the ideal, so too in a heathen family the parental relation failed to come up to the ideal, and yet the Apostle, without doubt, regarded that as the source of important and permanent obligations; and if he bade bond-servants to treat unbelieving masters with all honor (1 Tim. vi. 1), much more would he have recognized the duties of the natural relation of the child to the unbelieving parent.

The result then to which this exposition has brought us, is that Paul advances beyond our Lord's position in a single particular,—in conceiving of, and to a certain degree, authorizing separation without license of remarriage. That he goes so far is clearly shown by verse 11; that this leads him into any departure from our Lord's principles cannot, we think, be made to appear.

It will be seen in another place that the main stream of Protestant opinion runs in a direction contrary to that which we have pursued in regard to the sense of the Pauline passage in question, although we have the support of several of the ablest modern commentators. It will be seen also, that this opinion, not confining the Apostle's words within the limits of marriages where one of the parties was a heathen, but extending his principle so as to include all cases of desertion, has opened a wide door for divorce in Protestant countries.*

* For certain passages of the New Testament having a possible bearing on divorce, see note 1, in the Appendix.

CHAPTER III.

LAW OF DIVORCE IN THE ROMAN EMPIRE, AND IN THE CHRISTIAN CHURCH.

In the last chapter we attempted to set forth and explain the declaration of Christ and of the Apostle to the Gentiles on the subject of divorce. Our present object is to give a compendious view of the law of divorce in the Roman empire down to the time of Justinian, and of Christian opinion until it became the canonical law of the Catholic Church.

In the first chapter of our essay on divorce, we were able to do little more than allude to the legislation of Augustus, by which an effort was made to check some of the leading social evils of Rome, and which remained on the whole, ever afterward, the groundwork of Roman legislation respecting marriage. The emperor and his advisers were, without doubt, alarmed by the wide-spread violations of the rights of marriage, but to improve morals was not the only end they had in view. Population was beginning to decline; young men and old were averse to the marriage state, rather choosing to keep mistresses than to be encumbered with the expensive cares, and tried by the vexations of a family; and persons of the higher ranks preferred in some instances to marry freedwomen rather than the proud and costly descendants of the aristocracy. Hence it was enacted in these Julian laws that an unmarried man between twenty and sixty, and an unmarried woman or widow under fifty, should be debarred from sharing in inheritances or legacies, except where the testator was a very near relative. And, on the other hand, married men, especially those who had three children, enjoyed special privileges and honors. They had better seats than others at the public shows, they had advantages in obtaining office, and took precedence of their colleagues who had no such merit; they were exempted from certain burdens, and enjoyed certain rights of inheritance from which others were excluded; they incurred a milder penalty, when they had committed offenses calling for confiscation of property. Married women, too, who had borne three children, or, if freedwomen, four, had special privileges of their own in cases of inheritance, and were exempted from tutelage. It was enacted, also, to keep up the respectability of senatorial families, that senators and their sons should not marry freedwomen, play-actresses, or women of ambiguous character. Other men could ally themselves to freedwomen, and, as we have seen, when a patron contracted such a marriage, his wife, being his former slave, could not separate herself from him without his consent.

A very revolting part of the legislation of Augustus concerning marriage, was the legalizing of concubinage, as a state between lawful marriage and mere sexual intercourse. This was done, it would seem, in the hope of increasing population. This condition of life began and ended without formal notice or agreement; and the children had no legal father but only a mother. They therefore were incapable of being their fathers' heirs, but it would naturally happen that bequests would be made to them. Restrictions were put on the validity of legacies of this sort, by the early Christian emperors, on moral grounds, but Justinian took a milder course, and the way was open for the legitimation of such children. This relation between the sexes seems to have been very common under the empire, so that even free women of the better classes were found willing to take the place of concubines.* To the man it brought,

* A startling proof of this is given in the newly discovered work of Hippolytus, ix., § 12, p. 460, ed. Duncker. He charges Calistus, bishop of Rome, not only with ordaining men who had been married twice or thrice, and with treating a clergyman who had married after ordination as though he had not sinned, but with allowing women of rank, who were believers, to have a male concubine, slave or free, as they chose. Then, adds he, women called believers, began to secure themselves against having children by medicines procuring abortion, because, owing to their family connection and great property, they did not wish to have

as being a legal relation, no loss of respectability, and it was held to be more seemly for the patron to be united to his freedwoman by this tie than by that of a wife.

The legislation of Augustus, while it imposed penalties on adultery, and developed the principle of the retention of dower, left divorce as free as it was before. It could be brought about by common consent, or by action of one of the parties. Such action could be grounded on adultery of the other party,—and indeed the husband was now bound to put away a guilty wife—on *mores leviores* or more trifling offenses against the proprieties of the marriage relation, on various kinds of physical inability to fulfil the ends of marriage, among which madness without lucid intervals may be numbered, and on captivity. Of the incapacity of a freedwoman married to her patron to divorce herself from him we have before spoken. Of the effects of divorce on the speedier restitution of the *dos* or its partial retention, and of the trial of conduct by which the pecuniary liabilities of the two parties were determined we have no room to speak.

It has been maintained, we believe, that facility of divorce is necessary to prevent infractions of

a child by a slave or a low freeman. This Calistus was bishop in A. D. 217-221. Free women of the better classes were required on entering into this condition of life to make a *testatio* or formal notice of their intentions, and were liable otherwise to the penalties pertaining to *stuprum*.

matrimonial rights, but under the empire, although neither law nor opinion set up any strong barriers against divorce, adultery was exceedingly frequent. This appears from the strong assertions of poets and historians, and it is confirmed by facts. The crime burst out like a plague in the very highest classes. The grand-niece of the Emperor Augustus, Aquilia and Claudia Pulchra, members of distinguished families, Aemilia Lepida, wife of Drusus, who killed herself before trial, the sister of Caligula, his wife Livia Orestilla, Julia, daughter of Germanicus and niece of the Emperor Claudius,—these are examples from the history of the first four emperors of ladies tried and punished for this crime.* At the end of the second century an emperor of strictness and energy—Septimius Severus—endeavored to give effect to the laws against adultery, and Dion Cassius says, that, when he himself was consul, he found when looking over the register of cases that three thousand processes for adultery were instituted in this reign, but the war against manners was ineffectual, and the emperor, getting tired of his efforts on behalf of morality, stopped the prosecutions.†

The penalties for adultery‡ continued until the

* See Rein's Criminalrecht, 850–856.

† Dion Cass., 66, § 16.

‡ It may need to be said that only a crime to which a married woman was a party could be called *adulterium*. The Romans held that the *jus tori* pertained to the husband. He could not commit this crime against his wife.

time of the Christian emperors, much the same as they had been constituted by the laws of Augustus. The principal penalties we have already mentioned as being relegation and a loss of property. The woman convicted of the crime lost half her dower, and a third of her goods; and from her paramour half his property was taken away. They were banished to different islands. Besides these leading penalties the woman lost her right of marrying again, although she might sink to the condition of a concubine. She could no longer wear the matron's stole nor appear as a witness in the courts. The man also lost the right of testimony, and, if a soldier, was shut out from the army. The Christian emperors increased the severity of punishment for this offense, following herein, it would seem, the example of some of their predecessors, as well as influenced by the spirit of Christian morality. Constantine the Great imposed death with confiscation of goods on the *adulterer*. His sons punished the adulteress with burning and took away from her paramour the privilege of appeal, but this seems to have been only a case of extraordinary and temporary legislation. Under Valentinian the guilty woman was again sentenced to death. Justinian's legislation shut up the woman in a cloister, making it illegal for her husband to take her back within two years. If the parties were not reconciled at the end of this term the marriage was dissolved, and the woman's imprisonment in the cloister was perpetual. As for the offending man, he was visited with death, but not with confiscation of goods, if he had near relatives in the direct line.*

The legislation of Augustus in regard to divorce remained nearly unaltered until the times of Constantine. It was, however, a very feeble barrier against the disposition to break the marriage tie, and it read no moral lesson on the sanctity of that union. For, in the first place, it was a maxim of Roman law far down beyond the time when the emperors became Christian, that no obstacle ought to be put in the way of a dissolution of marriage caused by the free consent of the partners, liberty of marrying again being in this case equally unrestricted. The lawyer Paulus says, that it has been thought improper that marriages, whether already contracted or about to take place, should be secured by the force of penalty (*poenæ vinculo obstringi*), that is that two parties ought not to be forced by fear of penalty either to enter into a state of wedlock to which they were pledged, or to keep up such a state if they were agreed to the contrary. And it was laid down that marriage was so free, according to ancient opinion, that even agreements between the parties not to separate from one another, could have no validity,

* See Rein, u. s., 848–852, and Novell., 134, § 10, which renews Constantine's legislation.

(*pacta ne liceret divertere non valere*).* In the second place, the laws affected but a small part of the population of Rome. Slaves could contract no marriage. Concubinage became exceedingly common, it is probable, among the lower classes, and to this condition the law of divorce did not apply. The limited range of the law seems to be shown by the fact that for the legal formalities the presence of a freedman of the divorcing party was necessary. It is true that a freedman of a near relative was held to be essentially a freedman of the party giving the notice, but how many thousands of married people, or at least of Romans living together as man and wife there must have been, who could not provide a freedman for this formality. Did these classes furnish no cases of divorce, or were they overlooked by the law? We must conclude that they were never legally married, or that the law was intended to preserve a sort of decency of life in the upper classes, while the lower freemen were left to do as they pleased. Such was the freedom of divorce when it took place by the consent of both parties. It was equally free, a few cases only excepted,† where one of the parties terminated the union without the consent of the

* Paulus in Dig. xlv., 1, 134; Cod. viii., 39, l. 2, de inutil. stip.

† These were adultery,—where a man was obliged on penalty to dismiss his guilty wife;—the case of a freedwoman married to her patron who could not separate from him although he might from her; the captivity or insanity or certain bodily defects of one of the parties.

other, saving that here, if the woman had caused the divorce by her conduct, a large share of her dower was withheld from her, and if the man had caused it, he might be liable to pay over the whole of the dower, and that within a short term. The parties were subjected until the time of Justinian to a *judicium morum*, which might be instituted on a complaint of either consort. The fear, then, of losing a portion or the whole of the dower, and the dread of a loss of reputation, when the conduct of the parties in their married life should be investigated, seem to have been the only inducements to prevent one-sided divorces. But what if no misconduct could be alleged on the part of the man, what if he dismissed his wife to marry a richer woman, the law in this case had no restraining power. And where the wife brought no dower, as might happen in the lower classes, there could be no operation of the law at all.

It will not be strange if examples of the infamous freedom of divorce continued to occur through this period, until the first Christian emperor ascended the throne. Caligula sent away his wife and married another, whom he took from her husband on the wedding day, then after two months banished her from the city and united himself to a third, whom he dismissed on account of barrenness. Claudius repudiated four wives, and the fifth by taking poison escaped a similar lot. Nero and Domitian supply us with instances of divorce.

Elagabalus got rid of his first wife because she had a mole on her body, then, married a vestal virgin—an unlawful thing—and then after sending away a third, fourth, and fifth, returned to the vestal. But the doings of the miserable Carinus (about 284 A. D.), who married and divorced nine wives—*pulsis plerisque praegnantibus*, as the historian Vopiscus writes—are not easily matched, unless by the feats of those Roman ladies of whom Juvenal says, (vi. 229):

> "Sic fiunt octo mariti
> Quinque per auctumnos;

or that other in Martial's epigram, (vi. 7):

> "Aut minus, aut certe non plus tricesima lux est
> Et nubit decimo jam Thelesina viro."

Martial atones for many bad things by the words which follow:

> "Quae nubit toties, non nubit, adultera lege est."

But even Christian emperors practiced divorce, either on political grounds, as Honorius, or for private reasons, as Valentinian I. and Theodosius II., the latter because his sister and his wife were at variance.

With Constantine begins a strife between the stiffness of the principles of Roman law and the propensities of corrupt society on the one hand and the interests of religion and morality on the other. The vicissitudes of the contest show how hard it is to introduce legislation founded on higher principles into a demoralized society, half heathenish, and with unbroken precedents in favor of looseness in the marriage relations. Marriage had been a mere civil contract: the half-measures, the indirect ways of legislation, the ease with which they were overturned, from this point of time onward for more than two centuries, show that the world was still half, or more than half pagan. Christianity was doing something on behalf of humanity, something on behalf of justice, something on behalf of the sanctity of marriage throughout society, but we believe also that it could not have given new life to Rome, that when it shattered and dissolved the empire, this was a beneficent work, necessary for the greater sway of Christian ideas in future ages. It was the stone that was cut out without hands, and it smote the image upon his feet of iron and clay and brake them to pieces.

Neither Constantine, nor any of his successors before Justinian, attempted to interfere with divorces by consent of the parties. His legislation went no farther than to fix the cases in which the parties could without fault separate from one another. There were three for the woman, namely when the man was a homicide, a poisoner, or a violator of sepulchers; and three for the man, namely when the woman was an adulteress, a poisoner, or a procuress. This enactment belongs to the year 331. In 337 the wife had permission to put away her husband for the fourth reason, that he, being in the army, had given her no news of himself for four years.

If either of the married partners separated from the other without the justification furnished by the above-mentioned crimes, they were visited with penalties of a severity unknown before in similar offenses to Roman law. The wife who forsook her husband lost her dower "to the very last mite," and was banished to an island. The husband who sent away his wife without cause was bound to restore her all her dower at once, and was forbidden to marry the second time. Still further, if he thus married, his repudiated wife "could invade his house," as the law expresses it, and acquire possession of the entire dower of her successor. Of Constantine's penalties for adultery we have already spoken.

We add, as showing the spirit of legislation under Constantine, that he struck a side blow at concubinage by granting legitimacy to children already born in that kind of union, whose parents should contract legitimate marriage, and also by forbidding fathers to give any thing to such children or to their mothers in the way of donation or testament. But this last law was overturned by Valentinian I. and was not restored afterward in its full severity until the Emperor Leo, the philosopher (in Cent. 9), abolished concubinage in the East. Justinian extended the principle of legitimation introduced by Constantine to the children of concubinage in general. Such a tough life did this degraded caricature of marriage have, although abhorred by all the Christians in the world.

The divorce laws of Constantine were abolished by Julian (A. D. 363), who brought things back, as far as he could, into their old pagan channel. From that time for about sixty years there seems to have been no change in the law. Honorius, in A. D. 421, returned in a degree to the principles of Constantine's legislation, but united with them the old principle of Roman law, which Julian had recalled, of a one-sided separation for lighter faults, with retention of more or less of the dower. Theodosius II. in 439 abrogated earlier ordinances —probably those of Honorius—and after ten years of experiment, in which divorces had alarmingly increased, gave out another law, which laid down the causes for which one party might lawfully separate from the other. The woman was authorized to do this if the man had been guilty of certain crimes, among which are murder, poisoning, plotting against the government, fraud, and various sorts of robbery, cruelty toward or attempts on the life of his wife, intimacy with prostitutes, and adultery. The causes for which a man could without penalty put away his wife were for the most part of the same description with those just mentioned. But peculiar to her are the offenses of passing the night out of his house, or of visiting the theater, circus, or other public place against his will. Both the laws of Honorius and those of Theodosius had their penalties for unlawful divorce which we cannot stop to notice.

We go down to Justinian who, after tinkering on various occasions with this title of the laws, promulgated an important law in 536 (Novell. xxii.), and another in 542 (Novell. cxvii.). Of the last of these alone will our limits allow us to speak. This statute abolished for the first time divorce *ex communi consensu*, with the single exception that the married pair might give each other leave to go into a convent or take a vow of chastity. This was a most important step, and no Christian emperor had ventured to take it, although the contrary has, we believe, been asserted. As late as Anastasius, the second emperor of the East before Justinian, there seems to be no scruple about divorces by consent of the parties, and a woman so divorced is allowed to marry after one year.* This statute of Justinian

* This in fact appears from the law itself (Novel. 117, § 10), "Since many hitherto have dissolved marriage by agreement, we allow this to take place in no case hereafter," [except on account of chastity].—Comp. Cod. v. 17, l. 9.

It is remarkable that until the Novella 134 was issued in A. D. 556, there was no penalty attached to divorce *ex communi consensu*. Now the penalty for both parties was, to be shut up in a monastery and to lose their property. But if persons attempting to separate from one another in this way recalled their act be-again defined *the justifiable* causes of divorce, which were nearly the same as those that the law of Theodosius had laid down. In these cases the culpable party sustained a pecuniary loss by the separation, and might suffer also for his or her crime. Besides this kind of divorces, another, called divorce *bonâ gratiâ*, was allowed in special cases due to no fault of either party. The cases were impotence, captivity, and the choice of a monastic life—not by both consorts, which was provided for in another chapter of the law, but by either the wife or the husband. Lastly, there might be divorce without good reasons (*citra omnem causam*), which was visited with special punishments, especially with pecuniary loss.*

Some of the later laws prohibited remarriage to the party whose faults furnished ground for the divorce, or who dissolved the union without reason. The later legislation is also noticeable for another principle—the prohibition of marriage to a culpable party for a certain period.

This imperfect sketch is sufficient, perhaps, to present to our readers the leading features of divorce legislation under the empire. As a summing up of what has been said we remark:

fore going into the monastery, they might escape from these penalties. Agents in the transaction, such as notaries, were to be corporally punished and sent into exile.—Justin, in Novel. 140 (A. D. 566), restored divorce by common consent.

* See note 2 to chapter 3 in the Appendix.

1. That divorce *ex communi consensu* kept its ground all the way down to Justinian, and was attended with liberty of remarriage.

2. That divorce on account of adultery affected the dower and other property, and that the punishment of adultery increased in severity under the Christian emperors.

3. That divorce for greater or less fault of one of the parties was visited on the faulty party in the shape of retention of dower from the woman in whole or in part, and of payment of the dower in whole or in part by the man. At length some restrictions were put on the remarriage of the culpable partner.

4. Much the same may be said of groundless divorce in its consequences to the party which initiated it.

5. The Roman law during the empire did not to any extent prohibit divorce, but only made its consequences unpleasant; nor did it, except in a few cases, prohibit remarriage.

6. We see then that the influence of Christian views, which were already matured and vigorous in a theory of marriage, produced but little influence in changing the traditional principles of Roman law on this important department of the marriage relations.

But what were these Christian views in regard to divorce, which for a time conflicted with the principles of Roman law, and at length gained a victory over them? To understand fully the state of Christian opinion in this respect we ought to trace the doctrine of the church on marriage in general, from its beginnings derived from the Gospel or some other source, until it grew into a vast body of canonical law. But we have no room for such an exposition. We can only mention the sources to which this doctrine is to be referred. Of these there were two, a new conviction of the sanctity and closeness of the marriage relation, and a feeling that marriage, though a good and lawful state, was not the best or highest form of life. The conviction was founded on Christ's teachings and other passages in the New Testament, and on the spirit of Christianity which harmonized entirely with express declarations. Marriage now was God's ordinance, and at length was grouped together with some other important religious transactions of life in a class not very logically coherent, to which the name of sacraments was attached. The beautiful analogy traced by the apostle between Christ and the church on the one hand and the husband and wife on the other helped to secure for marriage a place among the sacraments.

But there grew up also at an early age of the church an opinion that a single life,—a life of chastity as it was called, just as many in the United States call abstinence from spirituous drinks a life of temperance, was best for the interests of the soul. This opinion was partly due to Gnostic or ascetic doctrines that crept in, partly it was a reaction against the deplorable licentiousness of heathenism, and it found a degree of support in passages of Scripture. Such were our Lord's words in Matthew xix. 12, several passages of Paul in 1 Cor. vii., and the place in Revelations, xiv. 4, where "virgins," understood of men, was supposed to commend celibacy. But the Fathers, as a body, held marriage in honor, as an institution of God. A Tertullian, after he slipped into Montanism, almost deserted this position, when he inveighed against second marriage as a sin. A Jerome writing against Jovinian, who had asserted that virgins, widows and wives, had equal merit, might say, "Si bonum est mulierem non tangere, malum est ergo tangere. Si autem malum est et ignoscitur, ideo conceditur, ne malo quid deterius fiat." But his logic came back to him when he grew cool, and in general the doctrine that marriage was an evil was left for heretics animated by an evil spirit "forbidding to marry."

To these sources, in whole or in part, must be ascribed the encouragement given to vows of virginity, to professions of widowhood, and to a solitary or social life of abstinence from marriage. Hence too the discouragement, in the case of laymen, of a marriage subsequent to the first, toward which such dislike was sometimes felt, that a Father of the second century could call second marriages, "specious adultery," and fourth marriages, together with third in some cases, were afterward prohibited by law in the Greek empire. Hence also the early ban put on second marriages of the clergy. Hence the long struggle against a married clergy, which in the western church was so far successful at length as to separate a married man wishing to become a priest from his wife, to make marriages after ordination void and punishable with a loss of office, and to extend the prohibition of them to all but the lowest servants of the church.* Hence, finally, the hindrances to marriage from blood and affinity, which reached in their operation to a wide circle of relations.

The doctrine of the ancient church on divorce was tolerably well established long before marriage came to be regarded as a sacrament in the more modern sense of that term. At the same time the sacramental character attached to marriage strengthened the view which Scripture authorized of its fixed and indissoluble nature. Even death was held by some, although never by the prevalent opinion, to be no dissolution of the bond. The original source of the doctrine was of course the declarations in the gospel, which were honestly and laboriously interpreted with a pretty

* Much as Jerome disparaged marriage, he freely admitted, as did most others, that any number of successive marriages was not unlawful. "Non damno bigamos, imo nec trigamos et si dici potest octagamos." Ad Pammach. Apologet. c. Jovin.

uniform result long before the doctrine of the sacraments was developed. This doctrine did not first teach the unlawfulness of dissolving the marriage tie, but took that view from the Scriptures and from the firm prevalent opinion already spread through the church. Afterward, however, the sacramental nature of marriage without doubt acted back to give more of rigor to marriage and to impede its dissolution. With this and before this the Christian spirit of forgiveness had an important influence on opinion in regard to divorce. The high sin of either party against the union might be repented of and God could forgive it. Why should not the parties be reconciled also? But for this it was necessary that they should remain unmarried. When forgiveness and restorations *ad integrum* became canonically lawful, there was naturally less need of relaxation in favor of a final separation with liberty of remarriage. These three then, Christ's law in the Gospel and as explained by Paul, the sacramental quality of marriage, the Christian duty of forgiveness, gave the shape to the doctrine of divorce in the ancient church. If the marriage had not been a Christian one, that is, had had no sacramental character, a complete divorce might take effect in the following cases, and in these only. In the *first* place an infidel converted to Christianity was to put away all his wives but the first. As however in this instance there was no true marriage according to Christian doctrine with any but the first wife, there was no real divorce in ceasing to have any relation to the others, who were merely concubines. *Secondly*, a converted infidel, who had put away his wife and married another, was required to take back again the first, even if she should have contracted a second marriage. Here again there was no true divorce, for the divorce and remarriage of both the parties was regarded as unlawful. *Thirdly*, if an infidel became a convert to Christianity, and his or her married partner was unwilling to keep up the marriage relation on any terms, or at least not without blaspheming God or leading the other into mortal sin, the Christian might be separated from the infidel so as to contract a new marriage.* This decision of the church was based on an interpretation of 1 Cor. vii. 15, concerning which we refer our readers to what was said in our last chapter. And here only have we an instance of true divorce. All other cases, such as marriage to a Jew of a person already a Christian, marriage of a Catholic to a heretic, or schismatic, either rendered the marriage void *ab initio*—which is not divorce in the proper sense—or merely justified a separation *a mensa et toro*, if even that were allowable.†

* The opinion of Innocent III. in the Decretals of Gregory IX., §§ 7, 8, de divortiis iv. 19, may be consulted here in lieu of every thing else.

† In the Greek church, marriage between the orthodox and

A very early and important passage on divorce is contained in the Shepherd of Hermas (ii. Mandat. 4, § 1). We will give it in English. "And I said to him, Master, let me ask thee a few things. Say on, says he, and I said, If any one had a wife faithful in the Lord, and found her in adultery, would the man sin if he lived with her? And he said to me, As long as he is ignorant, the man is without crime, if he lives with her. But if the man had known that his wife had offended, and the woman had not repented, and if she remains in her fornication, and the man lives with her, he will be guilty of her sin and partaker of her adultery. And I said to him, What then if the woman persist in her vice. And he said, Let the man put her away, and stay by himself, [*i. e.* remain un-

heretics was forbidden and declared null, although in Russia since 1719 members of the established church may marry members of other confessions. In the Latin church marriage with infidels or Jews has long been considered invalid. But for Catholics and baptized Protestants to intermarry is allowed, if they pledge themselves to educate the children in the Roman faith. Otherwise the priest may not celebrate the nuptials. But in modern times, even if such guaranties should not be given by the parties, the Catholic pastor may be present and record the marriage without blessing it; a singular compromise, as if the church were uncertain whether the transaction were concubinage or not. And in the Netherlands, since the papacy of Benedict XIV. (1740–1758), as well as in the western Prussian provinces since Pius VIII. (1829 onward), mixed marriages, celebrated not according to the form prescribed by the Council of Trent, but in one sanctioned by the law of the land, are regarded as real valid unions. (Walter, Kirchenr., §§ 300, 318).

married.] But if he put away his wife and take another, he too commits adultery himself. And I said to him, What if a woman, when put away, repents and wishes to return to her husband, shall she not be taken back by her husband? And he said to me, Verily, if her husband do not take her back, he sins, and allows himself to commit a great sin; he ought to take back the sinning woman who has repented; but ought not to do this often. For there is one repentance for the servants of God. On account of repentance therefore the man ought not to marry. This conduct is incumbent on both man and woman. Nor is there adultery only, said he, if one pollutes his own flesh, but also when any one does things like to the Gentiles he commits adultery. Hence, if one persists in such things also and repents not, withdraw from him and live not with him. Otherwise thou too art partaker of his sin. For this was the command given to you to remain by yourselves, whether man or woman, for in things of this sort there can be repentance."*

* In the Greek texts, as restored by Tischendorf, in Dressel's edition, and lately by Hilgenfeld, for "the sinning woman who has repented," of the Latin text, appears "him who hath sinned and repented." The words *there is one repentance*, etc., seem tc mean that only once and not more than once after baptism, a sin ner who has committed an act of open deliberate immorality can be received back as a penitent into the church. To give a sinning wife a motive for repentance and not to drive her to despair —this is what is meant by "on account of repentance a man ought not to marry" another woman. The indulgence of Hermas in

In this passage it is distinctly asserted that a man who puts away an adulterous wife, and marries another woman, commits adultery; and another reason is given for his remaining unmarried—namely that he may be in a condition to receive her back on her repentance. But such indulgence cannot extend beyond the first transgression. Here the foundation on which the first assertion is built is, no doubt, the words of our Lord, as limited by the Apostle in 1 Cor. vii., "let her remain unmarried, or be reconciled to her husband," and Hermas conceived that the reconciliation there referred to was to follow a separation on account of the adultery of the husband. He reasons fairly, as others have done then and since, that if this be a command for the wife, it is such also for the husband. Thus his injunctions are all scriptural, according to his understanding of Scripture. He may have been weak-minded, he may have misunderstood Scripture, as we think that he did, but he represents an opinion that must have been extensively held, and at length became the ruling one, and all this long before the doctrine of the sacramental character of marriage obtained currency.

allowing that there could be any second "repentance," was exceedingly distasteful to Tertullian, after he became a Montanist. Comp. his *de pudicitia*, §§ 10, 20, where he has the words "scriptura Pastoris quæ sola mœchos amat," and thinks that the author ought to have learned the opposite from the Apostles, referring to Hebrews vi. 4–6.

In the next three centuries many other witnesses appear on the same side. Clement, of Alexandria, says (Strom. ii., 23, § 144), that Scripture "regards marrying again to be adultery, if the other divorced partner is living;" and again, a little after (§ 145), "not only does he who puts away a woman cause her to commit adultery, but he who receives her also, as giving her opportunity to sin. For if he did not receive her, she would go back to her husband," where reconciliation is thought of as possible and desirable, whatever the woman had done to occasion the divorce. Origen seems to be of the same mind, where he says that some rulers of the church have permitted a woman to marry, while her husband is alive, contrary to what is written in 1 Cor. vii. 39, and Rom. vii. 3.* That Tertullian could be of another mind would be strange, when his opinion on second marriages in general is taken into account. In the fourth century, near the end, Augustin did more than any other man to establish the same opinion. He advocates it in several places. His treatise, *de conjugiis adulterinis*, to which we have already referred, was written especially to show that 1 Cor. vii. 11, "let her remain unmarried, or be reconciled to her husband," can be understood only of a wife who has withdrawn from her husband on account of his unfaithfulness, and he reasons pow-

* Origen on Matthew xix. 8, in the ed. of Lommatsch, vol. 3, p. 320. For Tertullian, see de Monogam., §§ 9, 10.

erfully, if inconclusively. His friend Pollentius had maintained that in this passage she was to remain unmarried, *quæ sine causa fornicationis discessit a viro*, thus interpreting it correctly, as Chrysostom did, of separation not amounting to formal divorce for causes short of the husband's crime.* Augustin maintains, as he had done many years before in his exposition of Matthew, that they were commanded to remain unmarried, *quæ a viris suis ea causâ recesserint, quæ sola permissa est, id est, fornicationis*. Pollentius thought also, consistently with this his opinion, that marriage is dissolved by adultery just as by death, and absurdly supported his cause by an appeal to Rom. vii. 2, "if her husband be dead she is no adulteress, though she be married to another man," on the ground that the criminal husband was to be regarded as if he were dead, and that therefore it was lawful *tanquam post mortem, ita post fornicationem conjugis, alteri copulari*. In this work Augustin comes on ground where Hermas stood. Thus he says to his friend, "what seems hard to you, that one of the married pair should be reconciled to the other after adultery, will not be hard if faith is there. For why do we still regard as adulterers those whom we believe to have

* Chrysost., Hom. xix., on 1 Cor. vii., where the causes of the separation, which the distinguished interpreter conceives of, are "continence, and other pretexts, and pettinesses," or comparatively trifling reasons.

been washed by baptism or healed by repentance?"

Jerome, a contemporary of Augustin, is also decided in his opinion on the same side, as may be seen in his commentary on Matt. xiv. 9.* A letter of his to a friend, Oceanus, is deserving of mention, as giving us the case of a divorce and remarriage of a Christian lady of high condition. Fabiola had a worthless, licentious husband. She had a right, says Jerome, to repudiate him, although not to marry again. The sexes ought to be equal in their rights. What is allowed to the man ought to be allowed to the wife. But Fabiola, young, rich, as yet not thoroughly Christian, thought, because her husband was rightfully put away, that she might marry another. She had not as yet known the "vigor of the Gospel," "*in quo nubendi universa caussatio, viventibus viris, feminis amputatur;* so while she avoided many wounds from the devil, she incautiously received one wound." The monk makes the best excuse for her that he can. "If she is blamed because when her husband was divorced she did not remain unmarried, I will readily admit her fault, while I ad-

* Ubicumque est igitur fornicatio et fornicationis suspicio libere uxor dimmittitur. Et quia poterat accidere ut aliquis calumniam faceret innocenti, et ob secundam copulam nuptiarum veteri crimen impingeret, sic priorem dimittere jubetur uxorem, ut secundam prima vivente, non haberet. Here, it would seem, if the crime was manifest and confessed, his objections against a second marriage would be nugatory.

mit her necessity." This lay in her youth, her position, her temptations. She married therefore, but after her second husband's death took such a view as Jerome and the times demanded, of her conduct. She openly professed repentance : *sic dolebat quasi adulterium commisisset.* She abounded in good works, and died, as Jerome thought, a most holy woman.*

From this time onward the rule became more and more established, that remarriage after separation was unlawful in the Christian Church, that only separations *a mensa et toro* were possible. The proofs of this are abundant, but they are needless, as the fact of a prevailing, and at length a universal opinion in the direction named is unquestioned.† No doubt the development of the sacramental theory contributed to the consolidation of this opinion. "A true marriage," says Innocent III., " can exist between infidels (*a matrimonium verum*), but between the faithful marriage is both true and fixed (*verum et ratum*), because the sacrament of the faith which is once received is never lost." And yet the teachings of the New Testament, as they were understood by the early church, gave this shape to the sacrament of marriage, so that as far as divorce is concerned,

* Epist. 77 of the Venice ed. of 1766.

† Consult the decree of Gratian, Caus. xxvii., Quaest. vii., a number of the Canons, Walter's Kirchenrecht, § 313, and the long note of Cotelerius, Patr. Apostol. 2, 88 (ed. Amstelod., 1724).

nothing essentially new was deduced from the sacramental theory.

While in the Western Church marriage became rigidly indissoluble, and civil law was shaped in conformity with ecclesiastical judgments,* in the East the case was otherwise. Some of the Fathers looked with indulgence on the remarriage of the innocent party, and, on the other hand, the law of the Greek Church permitted separation only when the wife and not when the husband had been unfaithful. But the civil law did not conform itself to the law of the Church and of the New Testament, as understood by the Church, but in some respects to the laws of Rome under the emperors. For a time even the principle of divorce by consent of the parties, which Justinian had abandoned, was again introduced. Remarriage was allowed somewhat freely, and to this legislation the practice in the church was accommodated.†

Nor ought it to be supposed that in the Western Church opinion in regard to the lawfulness of remarriage after divorce ran altogether in one direction. The "leaders of the church," to whom Origen refers in a passage we have cited, held that an innocent party might remarry when divorced on account of the adultery of a wife or

* "The stricter rule of divorce, on the ground of adultery alone, was first introduced into Italy [i. e. into state law] by Charlemagne and the Emperor Lothaire." Gans, Erbrecht iii., 180.

† Walter, u. s., § 315.

husband. Lactantius seems to hold the same where he expresses the Christian doctrine thus (Inst. vi., § 23), "that he is an adulterer who marries a woman put away by her husband, and he who, except for the crime of adultery, puts away his wife to marry another." So thought also the friend of Augustin, Pollentius, to whom we have adverted. Even Augustin had occasional doubts whether the innocent party, after putting away the adulterous one, might not marry again. In his treatise *de fide et operibus*, iv. 19, after saying that a man putting away a wife detected in adultery and marrying another ought not to be placed on a level with one who should do the same without the ground of adultery, he adds, "and in the expressions of the divine word it is so obscure whether he, who has an unquestionable right of putting away an adulterous wife, ought to be accounted an adulterer for taking another, that, as far as I can see, in this case any person may make a pardonable mistake (*venialiter ibi quisque fallatur*).* The same thing is taught so far as the innocent husband is concerned, by Ambrosiaster, as he is called, who is generally thought to be Hilary the Deacon. After citing 1 Cor. vii. 11, ending with, "and let not the husband put away the wife," he adds "except for the cause of fornication must here be

* Cited by Richter, Kirchenr., § 282.

understood. And for this reason Paul does not subjoin concerning the man what he had said before concerning the woman, because for the man it is lawful to marry another woman after putting away a sinning wife; for the man is not so bound by the law as the woman is, since the man is the head of the woman." From this reason, to say nothing of the conclusion, most of the church writers would entirely dissent. Thus Lactantius (u. s.) blames the one-sided Roman view of adultery, according to which "*sola mulier adultera est, quæ habet alium, maritus autem, etiamsi plures habeat a crimine adulterii solutus est.*" And Augustin held to the parity of the sexes in their marriage rights and obligations, saving that the sinning husband ought to be more heavily punished than the sinning woman.* To those who held the freer opinion that marriage was in one case dissolved, may be added the Council of Vermerie of the year 752, who decided that in case a woman could be proved to have plotted her husband's death, he might put her away and, if he desired, might marry another. Here the crime must have been regarded as equivalent to adultery.† But none of these opinions carried any weight with them, the stream of doctrine ran quite the other way, and at length the council of Trent only confirmed and reasserted what had

* De conjug. adult. i., 8, ii., 8.

† In the decree of Gratian, Caus. xxxi.. Quaest. 1, c. 6.

then been long admitted without dissent for ages, when it enacted the seventh canon on the sacrament of marriage, of which we gave the leading part in our last chapter.*

A word or two ought to be added in regard to the attitude which the church took toward the parties who had been separated from one another on account of crime. The marriage being dissolved only by death, the intention of the church was to excite repentance in the guilty partner, and after a probation to permit their reunion. The penance was a long one. In the time of Pope Stephen V. (Cent. 9) the husband could decide whether he would receive back a guilty wife after she had undergone seven years of penance or be separated from her altogether. To become thus reconciled was taught to be the duty of a Christian, according to the words of Christ, "neither do I condemn thee, go and sin no more." During their separation the pair were to have no intercourse as man and wife with one another; and for the violation of this rule a severe penance was inflicted on the innocent party. When the marriage was terminated by death and the adulterous partner was the survivor, Canon law was not so strict as Roman law. The adulteress for instance could now marry her paramour unless she had plotted against the life of her husband,

* See Appendix note 3.

or had promised marriage to the partner of her guilt during the life of her husband.*

We should now close our brief sketch of divorce, as it was looked at by the early and the mediæval church, were it not necessary to speak for a moment of another kind of transactions which are sometimes called divorces, but are quite unlike those of which we have been treating. We refer to the separation of parties who have been living together in marriage which is not really such, and who therefore, when thus disjoined by the proper authority, may be free to marry again. Such cases our Lord did not have in his mind when he gave out his law of divorce. But under every civil law there must be such cases. Under the canon law of the mediæval church there were many such cases. When they are brought before the court of the country or of the church it declares the marriage invalid; it pronounces a decree of nullity; it declares that the parties cannot lawfully live together hereafter, and possibly imposes penalties on them for so doing.

The canon law, which had marriage and divorce under its control, acted in regard to such cases as the Romans or any municipal law would. Its

* Comp. Decret. Gratian. Caus. xxxiii., Quaest. 2, c. 8, Caus. xxxi., Quaest. 1, several canons. Of course if the criminals were within certain degrees of relationship, there was another barrier in the way of their union. Caus. xxxiii., Quaest. 7, c. 19, 20.

peculiarity was the number and complication of these cases, and the snares which it laid, so to speak, for married persons by its strict rules of prohibited degrees. This again led to dispensations and to a gainful traffic in sacred things.

The impediments to marriage which went beyond putting off its solemnization, and which without vitiating the contract, did more than to render it improper for the priest to unite the parties in wedlock, were such as fraud, force, or serious mistake as the procuring causes of the consent, impuberty, impotence, a previous marriage, the vow at ordination or in entering a monastic order, difference of religion, and a certain closeness of relationship. The most of these we pass over in silence. By difference of religion is intended marriage of a believer with a Jew or an infidel, not marriage with a heretic or schismatic baptized person; and the case where one of two Jewish or infidel married partners becomes a believer is subjected to other rules founded on 1 Cor. vii. 12–16. The impediments from nearness of relationship, making or capable of making marriage void, grew up by degrees into a most intricate and cumbrous system from comparatively small beginnings. First the degrees of consanguinity within which marriage was unlawful were greatly extended. Next, on the principle that husband and wife are one flesh, the blood relatives of each were counted as relatives of both, and from this source might arise impediments to a second marriage of either of them. And not only this, but it became unlawful for certain blood relatives of the two parties to intermarry with one another. The rites of baptism too and confirmation introduced a spiritual relationship, as in the case of a godmother and a godson or his father, which was an obstacle in the same direction. So also adoption might present a hindrance of a similar kind.

In regard to consanguinity the canonical law went no farther at first than the Roman, which prohibited marriage between the immediate descendants of the same ancestor, as a brother and sister, and between one immediate and one more remote descendant, as an aunt and a nephew or a great-uncle and a grand-niece. In the reign of Theodosius the Great (A. D. 385), marriage between first cousins was forbidden. The church, starting from this point, gradually extended the prohibited circle until it included those who were within the seventh degree, that is, sixth cousins, according to a computation which counted the immediate descendants of a common ancestor the first degree, first cousins the second, and so on. This rule was authoritatively settled in the West in the eleventh century by Pope Alexander II. (A. D. 1065), although it had prevailed, more or less, long before. Being however not a rule of strict morality but of church practice, it could be dispensed with or suspended. Thus Gregory the

Great (A. D. 601) writes to his missionary in England, Augustin, permitting persons of the fourth and fifth degrees of relationship* to intermarry in that country, intending, as he says, that they should be, when more confirmed in the faith, bound by a stricter law. In this letter he makes the remark that Roman law allowed own cousins to marry, but says, "*experimento didicimus ex tali conjugio sobolem non posse succressere.*" But the rule of the seventh degree having been found inconvenient and not capable, *absque gravi dispendio*, of being observed, the sound sense of the great Pope, Innocent III., led him to bring about an alteration of the rule in A. D. 1215, at the fourth Lateran council. The new rule is this: *prohibitio copulæ conjugalis quartum consanguinitatis et affinitatis gradum non excedat*, which was so modified by Gregory IX. who had the decretals compiled, that a person in the fourth and one in the fifth, or third and fourth cousins, might be united in lawful marriage.† The same decree confined the ban of affinity to the fourth remove, which before had the same sweep with consanguinity to the sev-

* I. e. second and third cousins. See the passage in Gratian's Decree, Caus. xxxv., Quaest. 5, c. 2. It is Alexander's edict. The genuineness of Gregory's letter has been doubted. Compare Richter, § 168.

† A reason alleged for this was that *quatuor sunt humores in corpore, qui constant ex quatuor elementis*. Decretal. Greg. iv., 14, cap. 8.

enth degree. In the Greek Church the blood relatives of the married pair were considered to have contracted affinity with one another, but not in the Latin, except that the children of a woman's second marriage were looked on as standing toward her first husband's relatives within the prohibited circle, but this impediment again was taken away by the legislation of Innocent III. There was again an impediment from illicit intercourse which was brought within the narrowest limits by the Council of Trent. Still another from the relation of the godparent was so far removed by the same council, that it affected only the godparents, the child and its parents, and the baptizer. And the same analogy applied to the parties at a confirmation. Finally betrothal involved a ban against marriage for each party with the relatives of the other, but the Council of Trent restricted its effects to the first degree.*

In all cases, where a prohibition of marriage rested on other than fixed moral grounds, the pope, or others acting with derived authority, could dispense with the rules of the church, and this was done frequently, with or without reason. The Council of Trent makes the general order that dispensations are to be given beforehand either not

* Comp. Walter u. s. § 303–308, and Göschen in Herzog's Encycl. iii., p. 667 et seq. The leading canons may be found in the Decretals iv., 13 and 14, and in Sessio xxiv., cap. 2–4 of the Council of Trent.

at all or rarely, and, if at all, for good cause and gratuitously. There are to be no dispensations between parties standing in the second degree, *nisi inter magnos principes et ob publicam causam.* Another declaration of the council in regard to the extent of the dispensing power is worthy of notice here. "If any one shall affirm that only those degrees of consanguinity and affinity, which are expressed in Leviticus [xviii. 6, seq.] can prevent the contracting of marriage or separate it when contracted, or *that the church cannot give a dispensation in regard to some of them*, or enact that others besides shall not prevent and separate, let him be anathema." If the reader will consult the passage in Leviticus, he will find that all the cases there mentioned are beyond the precedents of dispensation, and would be regarded as obstacles of an absolute and moral nature, except that of *a brother's wife*, in verse 16. Is not this then a sort of ex post facto justification of the action in regard to the marriage of Henry VIII. with his deceased brother's wife?

When a marriage had been consummated with the proper formalities, and there appeared afterward good reason for believing that it was an unlawful one, the case was brought before an ecclesiastical court. Where the impediments were of a public character, a public authority alone could institute a process of nullity, but where the impediments affected especially the private interests of one of the parties, the injured party could bring a complaint. If a decree of nullity was given by the judge, it had no effect on the condition of the children, nor yet on that of the parties up to the time of the sentence, if they had acted with good faith; and in any case the form of the marriage protected the children. The parties after the decree were permitted to contract marriage with other persons, but the validity of the first marriage was always an open question, and new evidence might at any time reverse the decree. In this case the second marriage would be a nullity and the first would recover its obligatory force, so that now two separations, it might be, would be demanded by canonical law. The separations by sentence of nullity were formerly called divorces as well as the separations *a mensa et toro* on account of adultery, but a modern distinction of some Catholic writers between *annullatio* and *separatio* removes all ambiguity.*

We may sum up what has been said of the separation of married partners during the early and mediæval periods of the Christian Church in the following simple statements:

1. The prevailing and at length the unanimous opinion in the church was that no crime of either of the consorts, being baptized persons or Chris-

* Comp. especially Göschen in Herzog, u. s., 697–700.

tians, justified the other in marrying again during the life of the offending party.

2. When an infidel deserted his or her Christian consort, the latter was allowed to proceed to a second marriage.

3. The development of the theory of the sacrament, as far as divorce was concerned, accepted conclusions already drawn from Scripture.

4. As no crime entirely released the married pair from their relation to one another, and as forgiveness and reconciliation, being Christian duties, could now be exercised, consorts separated on account of adultery could come together again. For a time rigid penance kept the offender from the innocent party, and penance also was inflicted on the innocent party who strove to renew intercourse before the Church was satisfied.

5. In many cases where marriage was prohibited by canonical law, a sentence of nullity left them free to unite themselves to other persons.*

* Comp. Walter u. s. §§ 303-308, and Göschen in Herzog's Encycl., iii., p. 667 et seq. The leading canons may be found in the Decretals, iv., 13 and 14, and in Sessio xxiv., cap. 2-4 of the Council of Trent.

CHAPTER IV.

DIVORCE AND DIVORCE LAW IN EUROPE SINCE THE REFORMATION.

THE Catholic doctrine of marriage and divorce was settled long before the Reformation, and was only reaffirmed by the Council of Trent. The nations which retained their allegiance to the old church did not, so far as we are informed, make innovations in the law of divorce, but continue until now under the system handed down from the middle ages. Far different has been the history of legislation in most Protestant countries, and in that Catholic land which broke away at once from the old religion and from all faith in the Scriptures. The leaders in the changes of matrimonial law were the Protestant reformers themselves, and that, almost from the beginning of the movement. It will be our endeavor in this chapter to exhibit briefly the prevailing opinion at the Reformation in regard to divorce, and then to give a sketch of the law as it has shaped itself in some of the principal countries of Europe, especially in Prussia, France, and England.

The reformers, when they discarded the sacramental view of marriage, and the celibacy of the clergy, had to make out a new doctrine of marriage and of divorce. That doctrine was honestly derived from the words of Christ and of Paul. They saw, as they thought, in the rule of celibacy the source of boundless profligacy, a clergy all over Christendom living in secret sin and hypocrisy, or under the burden of a broken heart. They observed how the strict rules of the church were neglected in the case of the great by pliant priests, and how concubinage was almost tolerated. To this the doctrine that no crime dissolved marriage, that adultery only separated the marriage pair without giving relief to the innocent party, almost forced the church. Adultery, too, as a part of the same system, seems not to have been visited with severe church censures in the later centuries; we are led to judge that it was very common in the highest and the lowest classes; and to have an unfaithful wife was a matter to call rather for ridicule than for condemnation. The old Catholic theory of marriage, in short, was practically a failure in all its parts, in its ascetic frown on marriage, in its demand from the clergy of an abstinence not required from the Christian laity, in teaching that nothing but death could release a married pair from their obligations. When it sought for impracticable virtue, and forbade to some what God had allowed to all, it opened a fountain of vice with the smallest incitement to virtue. Besides this, it received, they thought, as far as divorce went, no countenance from the Scriptures. Christ had made a special exception allowing the innocent party to put away his wife on account of her crime and to marry another, while Paul, according to the interpretation of Chrysostom and his school, released, as they claimed, the deserted believer from all ties to his or her unbelieving partner. Thus they needed to have no fear of changing the law of divorce. Marriage, second marriage, marriage of priests had become honorable; marriage was no more a sacrament; why should its dissolution in cases provided for by the Scriptures be doubted? If to all this we add the minor considerations that Roman law, which allowed great freedom of divorce, must have grown in its authority as canon law became disregarded, and that the northern nations, where Protestantism spread, are probably less capable than the southern of being retained by such rules as the church had enacted, we shall have mentioned the leading influences which affected Protestant legislation on the subject of marriage and divorce.

The opinions of the reformers it is sometimes a little difficult to ascertain, as they seem to contradict themselves in different passages of their works. Thus Luther in his sermon on marriage, delivered at Wittenberg in 1525, uses the following language: "that [Matth. xix. 9] is a blunt, clear, plain text, which says that no one, either on account of leprosy or stinking breath or other defect, shall forsake his wife, or the wife her husband, except on account of whoredom and adultery. For only these causes separate man and wife. Yet it must be satisfactorily proved before separation, as reason demands, that adultery and whoredom have occurred." But in other places Luther's opinion is most openly expressed that malicious desertion may be followed by a divorce *a vinculo*. In an opinion of the year 1525, given to the council and clergy of Domitsch, he writes thus: "since a certain preacher's wife has dealt so dishonorably with him, I cannot make his rights longer or shorter than God has done, who through St. Paul, 1 Cor. vii. 15, in such cases pronounces the following decision: 'if the unbelieving depart, let him depart; the brother or sister is not bound in such cases.' So say I, too. Whoever will not stay, let him be off. The other party is not bound to stay unmarried, as I in a little book on that chapter have written more at large, to which I refer you. If, then, he cannot remain without a wife, let him wed another in God's name, because this woman will not be his wife." An opinion of 1535, signed by Luther, Cruciger, Major, and Melancthon, allows a woman of Nordhausen, whose husband had absconded several years before, to marry again, according to "the decision of Paul, and according to the former

6*

practice in Christendom, as a similar case cited by Eusebius from Justin, and the example of Fabiola show." The instances here adduced, by the way, are not in point, for they relate to adultery, and, moreover, Fabiola deeply regretted her step and is praised by Jerome for so doing.* Again, in his sermon "*von ehelichen Leben*," belonging to the year 1522, Luther mentions three causes justifying the dissolution of marriage, of which the first, existing already before marriage, is a reason for a sentence of nullity, and therefore has nothing to do with divorce proper; the second is adultery; the third is, "when one of the parties withdraws from the other, so that he or she will not perform marital duty, or lead a common life with the other." Thus, says he, "we may find an obstinate woman who stiffens her neck, and if her husband should fall ten times into unchastity, cares nothing about it. Here it is time for a man to say, 'if you won't, another can be found that will. If the wife will not, let the maid come.' Yet so that the husband give her two or three warnings beforehand, and let the matter come before other people, so that her obstinacy may be known and rebuked before the congregation. If she still will not, let her get herself gone, and

* The other instance is from Justin, *Apol.* ii. § 2, where a Christian woman divorced herself from a husband "who tried ways of pleasure against the laws of nature and against right." Nor is any thing said of her marrying again.

procure an Esther for yourself and let Vashti be off, as Ahasuerus did,"—a queer example without doubt to give to Christians. It is evident that here the refusal of connubial duty is thought of, although malicious desertion may be involved.*

The leaders of opinion in the Lutheran Church followed the first reformers in their doctrine of divorce. We cite but one,—Chemnitz—who in his examination of the Council of Trent, sums up a discussion on the sixth canon of matrimony in the following language: "We have, then, two cases in Scripture where the bond of matrimony is dissolved—not as by men, but by God himself. 1. On account of adultery a man lawfully, rightfully, and without sin, can repudiate his wife. 2. If an unbeliever will not cohabit with a believer but deserts, dismisses, and repudiates her, without charge of adultery, and only on account of her faith, the unbeliever sins indeed against God and against the law of marriage, but the innocent, deserted party is not under bondage, but is free from the law of her husband, so as not to commit adultery if lawfully wedded to another man. And these two cases Chrysostom also has noticed on 1 Cor. vii. 'Both unbelief,' says he, 'gives cause [for divorce] and so does fornication.'"†

* These passages are all found in Walch's ed. of Luther's works, vol. x. See pages 797, 886, 884, 721–727.

† *Examen Conc. Trid.*, ii. 430, of the Frankfort ed., 1615. We do not find the passage here cited in Chrysostom's Homily on this chapter.

Nor did the doctors in the reformed churches differ in their opinions or in their interpretation of Scripture from the Lutherans. Zwingli, in fact, with his characteristic audacity seems to have gone much farther than any one else. In the Zurich marriage ordinances of 1525, adultery, malicious desertion, and plotting against the life of a consort are not regarded as the only causes, but rather as the standard causes of divorce, and to the judge it is left to decide what others shall be put by their side. And not only this, but cruelty, madness, leprosy, are mentioned as causes which the judge can take into account.*

It seems to have excited some discussion in that age whether elephantiasis or leprosy—a disease then not so rare as now in Europe—could be a cause of separation from the bond of matrimony. Luther, in a passage already quoted, Calvin, in one of his epistles, and elsewhere, and Beza, in his treatise on divorce, all decide in the negative.†

The views of Calvin are somewhat obscurely expressed in his annotation on Matt. xix. 9, occurring in his commentary on the harmony. After speaking of the cause of divorce there contained in Christ's words, he condemns the opinion of those who hold elephantiasis to be another cause, "as

* Comp. *Herzog's Encycl.*, article *Ehe*, vol. iv., written by Göschen, professor of law at Halle.

† Calvin, *Epist.*, pp. 225, 226, of the Amsterdam ed. of his works, last volume.

being wiser than the heavenly master," and then speaks of the passage in 1 Corinthians in words like these: "When Paul mentions another cause, —namely that the believing brother or sister is not under bondage, where it happens that a consort is cast off by an unbeliever from a hatred of religion—he does not differ from the mind of Christ. For he does not discourse there on a justifiable cause of divorce, but only whether the woman remains bound to her husband when she has been impiously cast off from a hatred of God, and cannot return into favor but by denying God. Whence it is not strange that he prefers separation from a mortal man (dissidium cum homine mortali) to alienation from God." Here it might be said with reason that a case of desertion of a wife by an unsteady, dissipated husband, who had no objections to her religion, would not be covered by Paul's words, as Calvin interprets them. There can be, however, we conceive, no doubt that he would stretch his rule to include such cases. For the "ordonnances ecclésiastiques" of Geneva, enacted in general assembly, Nov. 20, 1541, some two months after his return from banishment, must have had his concurrence, and divorce *a vinculo* is there expressly allowed in cases of malicious desertion.* "If a man," it is there said, "being

* He returned from Strasburg, Sept. 13th, 1541, and the ordinances were passed Nov. 20th following, and went into effect Jan. 2d, 1542.

debauched, abandon his wife without the said wife's having given occasion or being culpable therefor, and this has been duly known by the testimony of neighbors and friends, and the woman has brought a complaint in demand of a remedy, let her be admonished to make diligent search in order to ascertain what has become of him, and let his nearest relations or friends be called to get news of him. Meanwhile, let the woman wait until the end of a year, if she cannot find out where he is, and let her commit herself to God. At the year's end she may come before the consistory, and if it appears that she needs to marry, let the consistory, after giving her exhortations, send her to the council to be sworn that she does not know where her husband has betaken himself, and let the same oath be taken by his nearest relatives and friends. After this, let such proclamations be made, as have been spoken of, in order to give liberty to the woman to marry again. If the absent man return afterward, let him be punished, as shall be judged reasonable."*

With Calvin, his disciple Beza agrees in his opinions concerning divorce. In his note, indeed, on 1 Cor. vii. 15, he says, "non hic conceditur divor-

* For this extract and for all other references to early Protestant church ordinances on divorce, we are indebted to a programme of Prof. Göschen of Halle, "doctrina de matrimonio ex ordinationibus ecclesiæ evangelicæ sæculi decimi sexti adumbrata." Halle, 1847. In his article, "*Ehe*" in *Herzog's Encycl.*, the same learned lawyer gives again some of the same matter.

tium, sed desertæ tantum consulitur," which might leave us in doubt how he explained Paul's words. But in his treatise, *de divortiis*, he examines the case spoken of by the Apostle, and having asked the question, Whether it is right for the deserted person, while the deserter is alive, to contract a new marriage, answers most expressly that she is entirely free to marry if she will. And in a letter to the churches of Neufchatel, in reply to the question whether leprosy is a valid ground of divorce, while he denies that it is, he reaffirms the doctrine taught in his treatise.*

The Protestant commentators of the sixteenth and seventeenth centuries, or the large majority of them, draw the liberty of remarriage after desertion from the word of Paul. Thus Paraeus: "she is free not only *a toro et mensa* but also from the marriage tie to the deserter." Aretius of Berne on Matth. xix.: "This one cause of lawful separation [viz. adultery] Christ lays down; but the Apostle on 1 Cor. vii. 15, allows another cause, arising from unequal marriage. Other causes, besides, we have pointed out in treating of the subject of divorce, to which we refer the reader."† So in century seventeenth, Grotius: "She is not bound to remain unmarried and to wait for or to seek for reconciliation. Christ's law is of force

* Beza *de repudiis et divortiis*, Op. ii. 94, 95, Genev., 1582, and *Epist.* x., in vol. iii., 215.

† He means apparently his *theologiæ problemata*, or *loci communes.*

when the parties are his disciples." Calixtus: "She is not bound to cohabit or to remain unmarried." Milton's views are well known. The Puritans seem to have followed this interpretation. But the interpreters within the English church were not all of this mind. Whitby, as nearly as we can understand him, is on the other side, and Hammond, who has no commentary on Paul's verse, in his paraphrase of it condemns marrying again in the case specified. Later still, we find several annotators of the eighteenth century disagreeing with the current Protestant interpretation.*

It is not strange that the ecclesiastical ordinances, which are platforms of discipline, and in some Protestant territories took the place of the old canonical law, by sanction of the civil power, should express the reigning opinion. A few of them, it is true, permit divorce proper for a single crime only: thus the "renovation" of the church in Nordlingen speaks thus: "In the matter of divorce we follow our Lord Jesus Christ, Matth. xix, not permitting true divorce, as far as it depends on us, except for the cause of fornication, nor without the production of witnesses and before a magistrate, that we may not, by furnishing occasion for fraud, add the force of malice to evils already existing. But in other things we follow the Apostle Paul, 1

* See Wolfius, *Curæ philolog.* on the passage in Corinthians, where they are spoken of at large.

Cor. vii., and allow persons who seek a divorce to be separated by authority of the magistrate, but on condition that they remain unmarried, according to the precept of Christ, Matth. xix." So the "church-order of the Netherlanders at London" (1550): "from all these words of the Lord one may easily perceive that the marriage bond is exceedingly strong, and that it can be broken only by death and whoredom." So the "sacred liturgy of the church of the foreigners at Frankfort" (1554)* says that "they whom God has joined together, can never be separated but on account of fornication, or for a time by mutual consent, that they may give themselves to fasting and prayer."

But the great majority of the ordinances add malicious desertion to adultery as a second ground of divorce. So those of Lübeck (1531), of Goslar (same year), of Lippe (1538), of Geneva, already mentioned (1541), Calenburg-Göttingen (1542), Brunswick-Lüneberg (1543), Brandenburg (1573), Mecklenburg (1570), Brunswick-Grubenhagen (1581), and Lower Saxony (1585). The last but one of these uses the following words: "By no means shall any divorce be allowed or procured except in two cases which Christ and Paul have allowed in the gospel. As namely and in the first place, when one of the parties has been satisfactorily proved guilty and jurally convicted of adultery,

* That is, as we suppose, the church of the English, which had its difficulties in that year.

and the innocent party will not or cannot at all become reconciled to him, in such case at length the sentence of divorce shall be pronounced according to Christ's words, Matth. xix. . . . In the second place, in cases of malicious desertion, running away and abandonment, of which St. Paul speaks, 1 Cor. vii." And the last-mentioned ordinance says that "whatever besides these two causes [adultery and desertion] has been brought in by some emperors, as Theodosius, Valentinian, Leo, Justinian, to justify divorce, cannot be sufficient for that purpose."*

One or two only of the ordinances of this period extend the permission beyond the two causes of divorce so often spoken of. Those of Zurich we have already mentioned. A Prussian consistorial ordinance, in cases of cruelty after fruitless attempts to reform the man by discipline, allowed a separation from bed and board not exceeding three years, after which the parties might be united again, on the offender's giving sufficient security that he would not repeat his misdeeds. If after this, there should be an attempt by either party on the other's life, by poison or otherwise, they might thereupon be divorced, and the guilty party be remitted from the matrimonial to the secular court.

The question was discussed among the reformers whether the adulterous party ought to be

* All these instances are from Prof. Göschen's programme.

suffered to marry again during the life-time of the other consort. Luther insists with great energy that death ought to be the penalty for adultery, but since the civil rulers are slack and indulgent in this respect, he would permit the criminal, if he must live, to go away to some remote place and there marry again. So Calvin, in several places, declares that death ought to be inflicted for this crime, as it was by the Mosaic code, but if the law of the territory stop short of this righteous penalty, the smallest evil is to grant liberty of remarriage in such cases.*

The church laws of the seventeenth and eighteenth centuries in Germany very generally concede divorce only in the two cases already named,

* Luther's words are (Walch, x. 724), "but if the civil authorities are slack and negligent, and do not kill the adulterer, he may flee to a distant land and there marry, if he cannot be continent. But it were better he were dead and gone, to prevent evil examples (aber es wäre besser todt todt mit ihm, etc.)."

So Calvin in a letter (Epist., p. 225, Amsterd. ed. of his works, last vol.) says that "because the punishment of adultery has not been as severe as it ought to be, so that they do not lose life who violate the faith of wedlock, it would be hard that [a man or woman who had thus sinned] should be prohibited from marrying during life-time. Thus it is necessary that one indulgence draw with it another. Yet it seems wisest not to let the guilty woman do as she will in regard to marrying at once. Such permission should be delayed, whether by prescribing a certain time or by waiting until the innocent party has contracted a new marriage." In his note on Matth. xix. 9, Calvin expresses the same opinion in regard to the deserts of the adulterous wife or husband, and the "perverse indulgence of magistrates."

but the Wirtemberg ordinance goes farther than this; it adds as grounds of divorce impotence supervenient on marriage through the fault of one of the parties, and obstinate refusal of matrimonial duty.

Meanwhile, a new turn was given to opinions concerning divorce toward the end of the seventeenth century. Thomasius (ob. 1728), a professor of law at Halle, an audacious but superficial thinker, gave the direction by leaving out of sight the religious and moral side of marriage, and looking at it only as a civilian.*

He had vast influence on his age and many followed in his steps. Thus Kayser, afterward a professor at Giessen, in a disputation of the year 1715, regards as good grounds for divorce, incompatibility of temper, contagious disease, cruel treatment, irreconcilable animosity, and other grounds rarely or never held to be sufficient before. Marriage is now coming to be regarded as a contract for attaining merely outward ends, as an institution to be shaped and modified by the state, according to its views of expediency and its opinions as to the best means for securing civil happiness; it is putting off its religious and moral character.

These new views, which tallied so well with the shallow spirit of the eighteenth century, found

* For Thomasius, see Tholuck's Article on him in *Herzog's Encyclop.*, vol. xvi., and his "Preliminary History of Rationalism," ii., 2, 61–76.

their expression first in the legislation of Prussia.* In 1749, 1751, part of a project of general code for the Prussian states was published by Cocceii, the chancellor under Frederic the Great, and the divorce regulations which formed a portion of this project, although this, as a whole, never acquired a legal existence, passed by degrees into the law of a large number of the provinces composing the Prussian kingdom. In this project the innovations are chiefly the following: first, that consent of the parties can dissolve marriage, although a term of a year's separation from bed and board is required to give opportunity for reconciliation. Should they at the year's end still persist in their decision, divorce may now be granted. Secondly, divorce is allowed on account of "deadly hostility" between the parties, and is made to depend on a variety of indications, as when blows are given by one of the parties, or he has an infamous disease, or he plots against the life of the other, or is condemned to an infamous punishment. To this, it is added, that complaints may be made for smaller faults, as the cruelty (sævitia) of the husband, the extravagance or drunkenness of the wife. Here, too, a probation of not more than a year's separation must precede a sentence of full

* For the legislation anterior to the introduction of the Prussian Code or "*Allgemeines Landrecht.*" we rely on an Essay by Savigny, entitled "Reform of the Laws concerning Divorce," in his Miscell. Works (Vermischt. Schrift.), v. 222–414.

divorce. One of the provinces, a little after, did away with this probation in the case of "deadly enmity," and authorized divorces on this ground to be granted at once.

Then came a reaction. The king—still Frederic the Great—while on a journey in Pomerania, in 1782, had his attention drawn to the frequency of divorces, especially in the lower classes. He therefore issued an edict complaining of the frivolity with which divorces were sought, the readiness to contract inconsiderate marriages, the evils to families, etc.; and the chancellor was required to amend the legislation. In the edict published in consequence of this movement, divorce by consent of parties was restricted to cases where the marriage had been without children for several years, and the judge was to be satisfied that the divorce was sought by both parties freely, and after mature consideration. Divorce for fault of one of the parties is granted on account of those same crimes and differences between the parties, which the law of 1749 regarded as justifying reasons. Soon after this a project of a general code was made, out of which the code of 1791 grew. Here divorce by mutual consent is admitted only when the parties have been four years without children, or when for other reasons there is no prospect of any. Divorce for deadly hatred is still admitted, but the law adds that no marriage shall be dissolved on account of invincible disinclination avowed by one of the parties. The proofs of hatred as they appear in former laws are now made distinct grounds of divorce from the hatred itself.

We next come to the code or "Landrecht" which is still in force for the kingdom of Prussia.* Here the grounds for divorce involving wrong of one of the parties are, first, adultery, sodomy, and other unnatural vices, and suspicious intercourse, especially after prohibition by a judge, attended with a violent suspicion of adultery (668–676). Next comes malicious desertion, of which quite a number of cases are given. For example, if a woman leave her husband without cause, the judge may require her return. If she refuses, her husband may sue for divorce. A husband is not bound to take back a wife who has left him until she proves the correctness of her life while away. If a person is away on urgent and lawful business, his act is not desertion exactly, but his consort must wait ten years, and then sue for a judicial declaration of his death (676–693.) Persistent refusal of marriage-intercourse is regarded as equivalent to malicious desertion (694–695). Plots or practices, endangering the life or health of the other party, together with gross injury to the honor or personal freedom of the same, are sufficient grounds for divorce. But persons of lower condition shall not have divorce granted to

* Preuss. Landrecht, II., part I., chiefly §§ 668–834. We quote the sections.

them on account of threats or abuse with the tongue, nor for injurious acts and outrages, unless these are causeless and maliciously repeated. Incompatibility of temper (unverträglichkeit) and quarrelsomeness are good grounds only when the innocent party's life and health are endangered (699–703). Gross crimes, for which a disgraceful punishment is suffered, furnish ground for divorce. So, also, when one party falsely accuses the other of such crimes, or intentionally puts the other in danger of losing life, honor, office, or business, or enters into a disgraceful employment (704–707). Drunkenness, extravagance, or a loose manner of life (unordentliche wirthschaft) may be followed by divorce, if not corrected by steps which the judge takes on application from the innocent party (708–710). So also failure to support a wife, caused by crime, dissipation, or loose living, entitles her to divorce, when after arrangements made by the judge for her divorce the husband persists in his conduct (711-713). In all cases the judge must take pains to restore a good understanding between the alienated parties (714).

The causes for divorce which may be referred to accident or visitation of providence are these: incurable impotence supervenient after marriage, together with other incurable bodily defects exciting disgust or preventing the fulfillment of the ends of the marriage state (696–698), and insanity lasting over a year without prospect of cure (698).

The causes depending on the will of both or of one of the parties are these: "Marriages without children can be dissolved by mutual consent, if neither frivolity nor haste nor secret force on either side can be discovered. But mere disinclination of one party toward the other, not sustained by positive acts, is ordinarily no cause of divorce, and yet in special cases it may become such, where the alienation is deep, violent, and irreconcilable." But in such cases the party urging this plea against the other's will must be declared to be in fault, and is liable to the penalties, or disadvantages in regard to property, spoken of in a subsequent portion of the law (716–718.) Where the reasons alleged for divorce are of less weight, and hope of reconciliation exists, the judge can delay making known his sentence for a year, pending which time the parties may live separated, and the judge must decree in regard to questions of property and children. At the end of the term a new attempt at reconciliation must be made, and if this is ineffectual, sentence can then be given (723–731).

No divorce shall be granted where one party has brought the other to the commission of the misdeeds on which the complaint is based. So condonation is an estoppal to suits arising out of the crime forgiven. Cohabitation for a year after knowledge of the crime implies condonation.

No separation from bed and board is allowed if

one of the parties is a Protestant. If both are Catholics, such separation has all the civil effects of divorce. And it is left to the consciences of the parties concerned to decide what use they will make of their separation in the matter of contracting new marriages (733–735).

The *consequences* of divorce form an important branch of the Prussian law. Divorced persons may in general marry again whom they will. But a person divorced for adultery may not marry the partner of the crime. Nor may they who have been divorced on account of suspicious intercourse marry those who have been connected with them in their suspicious acts, and have produced a variance between the consorts (25–27). Divorced persons, like others, contracting a new marriage, must prove the dissolution of the old one to the clergyman who publishes and solemnizes the nuptials (17), and if there are minor children of a former marriage, must exhibit a legal composition with them in regard to property, or at least a permit of a court of wards, before the new union can be celebrated (18). As for the rest, no delay is imposed on the divorced man's remarrying, but the woman must wait according to circumstances, from three to nine months (19–23).

In the bearing of divorce upon the property of the parties, the Prussian law seems to have followed to some extent the provisions of the Roman code. At the time of the process it must be determined by the judge which party is to blame for the divorce, or which is more so, if both are in fault. Wrongs directly violating marriage duty are more blameworthy than such as do this indirectly. Intention also, and lightness of mind must be taken into account in reckoning the fault. This being ascertained, the case may be that neither party is declared guilty, or that one is or is principally so, and provisions are necessary, according as the property was held separately or in common. In the first case, where neither party is pronounced guilty, and the goods were not held in common, they follow the rules prescribed for separation by death. If there was a community of goods, each takes the part contributed by him or her to the common stock before marriage, or added since. But in the case of persons from whom a divorce is obtained on account of certain visitations of Providence, the other party—the sane party for instance—must support the unfortunate one according to their condition in life, if the latter has not the means of support in his own hands. In the other case, where one of the parties is pronounced guilty, the rules in regard to the division of property run into details too long to be described. The general principle is that the guilty party, whether husband or wife, shall suffer in property, as a sort of compensation to the other for crime or indiscretion. Thus, if no community of goods had existed, the party whose conduct caused the divorce is considered civilly dead, and all the advantages conceded by the law to a surviving consort are granted to the innocent partner. If community of goods had existed, the innocent party can choose whether to take half of them, or to demand a division. If they are divided, the portion of the guilty party is liable for the same satisfaction or compensation, as if there had been no community of goods. This satisfaction, if divorce grew out of the grosser offenses named in the law, and there had been no bargain, amounts to one-quarter of the property of the guilty party, and if the offenses were less gross, to one-sixth. Instead of this satisfaction, the innocent wife can demand alimony on a scale suitable to her condition in life. And if the innocent husband, through age, sickness, or misfortune, is not in a condition to earn his living, he can, instead of a satisfaction, choose alimony to be paid out of his wife's property. But if the guilty party can give neither compensation, nor satisfaction, nor support, he or she must for the offenses occasioning the divorce be imprisoned, or be put to penal labor, for a time varying from fourteen days to three months (745–823).

Marriage in Prussia, as in most other Christian countries, requires certain religious formalities in order to be valid. If a Catholic curate hesitates to publish and solemnize a marriage allowed by the laws, because the dispensation of his superior has not been asked for or has been refused, he must allow another clergyman to perform these services in his place. For Protestant ministers there is, we believe, no such indulgence. And hence, those who regard the Prussian law of divorce as heathenish and unchristian, who scruple to unite a woman divorced without adultery to another husband and to say that God has joined them together, must occasionally be brought into extreme perplexity. The only way of preventing such outrageous tyranny is to put them on a level with Catholic priests, or to introduce the French civil marriage.

It is natural that the complaints against the Prussian law should be great. Not only has it dissatisfied numbers of the clergy, but some also of the most eminent jurists have desired to see it modified. Savigny (u. s. 353-414) gives us two such documents, containing projects of new divorce laws framed by two commissions, the one in 1842, the other in 1844. He must have been in the counsels which originated one or both of these. We have no room to describe their provisions, except to say that they both exceedingly abridge the causes of divorce. Both pronounce against mutual consent, violent contrariety of temper, deficient proof of innocent life on the part of a woman separated before divorce from her husband, disease and defect caused after marriage by visitation of Providence, and suspected intercourse contrary to the order of a court. Besides these, the first commission of 1842 eliminates madness, refusal of connubial duty, injuries to the honor or freedom of one of the parties by the other,—unless they run into prolonged and gross outrages,—quarrelsomeness, danger to life, honor, office, or business by unpermitted actions, unless these furnish reason for divorce of another kind; together with drunkenness and other loose living, and failure to furnish support, excepting the case when through crime, drunkenness, or dissoluteness a man has taken away from himself the power to maintain his wife, in which case divorce may be allowed. It is a decisive condemnation of the law that jurists of the highest eminence were found ready to make such sweeping changes in the code. But the attempts to change the law were ineffectual, nor have others since made, unless we are deceived, been more successful.

The provisions of the Austrian code applicable to non-Catholics and the church-ordinance of Baden approach nearest in point of laxity to the Prussian law. All the other States of Germany confine divorce to cases of guilt, although they generally go, in their enumeration of the kinds of wrong-doing which furnish ground for divorce, beyond the legislation of the age of the reformers.

From Prussia we turn to France, where the experiments in divorce legislation coincide nearly with the phases of political revolution. The old system, conformable to the ecclesiastical law of divorce, was overthrown by a new divorce law passed

Sept. 20, 1792, at the opening of the National Convention. In this new law three causes of divorce are allowed, mutual consent, allegation of incompatibility of temper brought by one of the consorts, and certain specific or determinate motives derived from the condition or conduct of either of the married parties. These last are derangement of reason, condemnation by a tribunal to a painful or infamous penalty, crimes, cruelties, or grave injuries of either party toward the other, notorious licentiousness of morals, desertion for at least two years, absence for at least five without sending news, and finally emigration from France in certain cases, which was naturally a transitory measure. Separation of body, or divorce *a mensa et toro*, was to be hereafter abolished, and separations already decreed by process at law could be turned into divorces. The divorced parties could marry one another *de novo*, and could marry other persons after a year, in cases of divorce for incompatibility or with mutual consent. When the divorce was granted for a determinate cause, the wife must wait a year before marrying, except in the case of the husband's absence for five years, when she is allowed to marry immediately after obtaining her divorce.

So far the new law went back to the loose Roman practice, but the mode of procuring divorce was somewhat original. In case the steps for this purpose began in mutual consent, a family council of at least six relations or friends was to l convened by the parties, half chosen by the husband, half by the wife. When after a month's warning the council should meet, it was to hear the reasons of the parties who had desired divorce, and to make observations on the case. If not reconciled, the parties were now to present themselves, from one to six months after the meeting of the council, before the proper public officer of the husband's domicil, who, without entering into the reasons of the case, was to grant the divorce. If the parties neglected to take this step within six months after the meeting of the council, they would need to go through the same formalities again after the same intervals. If they were minors, one or both, or had children, the delays were to be doubled.

In cases where one of the consorts demanded divorce on the ground of incompatibility of temper, the steps were the same as those already described, with this difference, that there were to be three assemblies of the family council at certain fixed intervals.

Where a specific ground for divorce was alleged by one of the parties, if it were absence without news for nine years, or judgment for crime, the public officer could grant the suit at once, unless indeed the nature or validity of the judgment were contested by the other party, in which case the tribunal of the district must first decide the disputed point. If the specific ground were any other, as derangement, profligacy, desertion, injury of the consort, the demandant had first to bring his case before family arbitrators "in the form prescribed for suits between husband and wife." If they regarded his demand as founded in fact, the divorce could be granted by the public officer of the husband's domicil, but there might be an appeal by the defendant from the arbitrators' sentence, which appeal was to be decided within a month.

This law opened a wide door to divorce, and in so doing disregarded the feelings and habits of the devout Catholics still remaining in France, by banishing all separation *a mensa et toro* from legislation. But the door was not yet wide enough for a "wicked and adulterous generation." It needed the additional clauses passed by the National Convention on the 8th of Nivôse, An 2—Sat., Dec. 28, 1793—and on the 4th of Floréal of the same year—Wed., April 23, 1794—to become perfect of its kind. The first addition, brought forward by Merlin of Douai, who said that it was conformable to a provision of a civil code then in the hands of a revising committee, enacted that a divorced husband might marry immediately after the divorce was pronounced, and the wife after an interval of ten months. The second, a far more immoral enactment, declared that a separation in fact of a married pair for six months, even though proved by common fame only, should be cause for pronouncing them divorced without delay, if one of them demanded it. The document certifying such common fame should be given by the council of the commune on the attestation ot six citizens. The demander of the divorce, if a resident for six months in a new commune, could cite the other partner before the public officer of his actual domicil. But no citation was necessary, if one of the pair had abandoned the commune where they lived without giving news of himself afterward. The divorced woman could marry after a certified separation in fact of ten months, but an accouchement in the interval would render such delay unnecessary. Finally, divorces effected and authenticated before Sept. 20, 1792 [and therefore with no law to authorize them], on the ground that marriage is a civil contract, are confirmed in their legality.

These final strokes of the law belong to the worst times of the revolution. A reaction showed itself in the autumn of 1794, and these two last laws were suspended on the 15th of Thermidor, An 3,—Sunday, Aug. 2, 1795. The representative Mailhe, who moved the suspension, remarked that by these laws the hasty outbursts of passion became irreparable, and took from their unhappy victims the refuge even of reflection and repentance. He then goes on to say that the law of 4th Floréal, making separation in fact for six months a ground of divorce, was forced on the legislative committee of the Convention by a "decemvir," meaning, we suppose, a member of the Committee of Public Safety, who had under his protection the wife of a man shut up in one of the "bastiles of terror," and wished to secure her for himself without loss of property, which would be sequestrated if her husband was condemned before her divorce.* "A decree of exemption might have unmasked this new Appius. It was thought better to propose a general law." "You know in fact," says he, "that the decemviral oppression weighed on the committees, and on the Convention generally. Into how many families have not these laws [of 8 Nivôse and 4 Floréal] brought dissolution and despair. How much at this moment do they not aggravate the condition of those who are detained for reasons of general security [who may be separated in fact six months by imprisonment, and so lose their wives by these laws]. You cannot too soon stop the flood of immorality which these disastrous laws are rolling on us."

Thus the law of Sept. 20, 1792, alone was now in force, and continued to govern in cases of divorce for some eleven years.†

The last form which the law of divorce took in

* We are not sure that we have seized the sense here.

† The laws mentioned above may be found in the "réimpression de l'ancien Moniteur," generally a few pages after the date of their enactment. The remarks of Mailhe we have extracted from the same journal. See Vol. 19, 69; 20, 297; 25, 403.

France before the restoration of the Bourbons, was that which appears in the Code Civil des Français, or as it was subsequently called the Code Napoléon. From the year eight of the Republic, corresponding with parts of 1799 and 1800, a project of a code had been sent to the superior courts for examination, and then—their observations being placed in the hands of the Council of State—the section on legislation within the council made a new project, which, after discussion in the council, resulted in the *Code Civil.* These discussions are of high interest, as indicating a reaction from the views of the revolution concerning divorce, and we should be glad to quote from them at large if we could afford the space.* The title on divorce was decreed March 21, 1803, or 30 Ventôse, An 11, and continued to be law until the fall of Napoleon, with very slight changes due to the imperial system. The differences between this law and that of Sept. 20, 1792, are chiefly these. The system of family councils is abandoned. The formalities in cases of divorce by consent of both consorts, or complaint of one, are such as to retard the decision considerably, and give time for reflection and the spirit of reconciliation. The limits within which divorce by mutual consent is confined show

* We use the "discussions" as arranged by Jouanneau and others according to subjects. Paris, An xiii. (1805). The chief speakers are Portalis, Boulay, Berlier, Emmery, Tronchet, the First Consul Bonaparte, and the Consul Cambacérès.

a feeling that the license in this respect had gone too far. In case of adultery the offending party could contract no marriage with his or her partner in guilt, and the adulterous wife was subjected to confinement in a house of correction. A divorced couple could never be united together again in marriage. Separation "*de corps*" or *a mensa et toro* is restored to legislation for the sake of the Catholics.

A long discussion took place in the Council of State on the question whether incompatibility of temper, or in other words mutual consent should be admitted at all as a ground of divorce. The distinguished lawyer Portalis was against divorce for incompatibility of temper. There was no reason for it in the nature of marriage as a contract. This was not an ordinary contract. No legislator would endure such a thing as a marriage for a limited term of years. It subsisted for society, for children; and the interests of the wife repelled divorce for indeterminate reasons. The granting of such divorces multiplied their number, and tended to demoralize France. Others agreed with him, and all the tribunals had been of the same opinion, or like that of Paris, had demanded that the incompatibility should be proved by facts. The First Consul, whose vigorous thinking is continually manifest, replied that mutual consent was a way of hiding shameful family secrets from the public gaze. Tronchet replied that the malignant would say that the pretext of incompatibility had been employed to conceal more shameful reasons. Portalis, too, said that a wife would say to the legislator, "you dishonor me by concealing the true cause of the divorce; you give room to all sorts of suspicions; whilst my husband who repudiates me quits me only because he is hurried away by a shameful passion." "And what inconvenience," adds he, "would there be in accusations for adultery being made public. It is the crime which makes the shame, and not the accusation. If we look within we shall find that the only fear that agitates us is that of ridicule; for, we must confess it, in the present state of our morals we seek to save ourselves more from ridicule than from vice itself." These views did not prevail. The council, notwithstanding the arguments against mutual consent as a ground of divorce, introduced it into the law; and principally for the purpose of covering up specific causes of divorce, which it might be disgraceful to have known. Some of those who were consulted in framing the law proposed that this kind of divorce should be interdicted to consorts who had children, but the proposal was rejected—one member of the council remarked that children were thus spared the shame of having the scandalous conduct of either parent spread abroad.

To come now to the law itself (Code Civil, Tit. VI., Art. 229–311), the causes of divorce are the following: 1. for the husband, the wife's adultery; 2. for the wife, that gross form of the husband's adultery when he has kept a concubine in the common dwelling; 3. for either consort, outrages, cruelties, or grave injuries inflicted by the other (excès, sévices, injures graves); 4. for either, the condemnation of the other to an infamous punishment (peine infamante). 5. "The mutual and persevering consent of the consorts expressed in the manner prescribed by law, under the conditions and with the proofs which it establishes, shall be sufficient evidence that a common life is insupportable to them, and that there exists in their case a peremptory reason for divorce."

These grounds for divorce are divided into determinate or specific, and indeterminate, or those which rest on no specific act or series of acts. In assigning these grounds the law stops short of the freedom of the Roman law, which it in some respects follows,—for instance, in making ordinary adultery on the part of the husband no cause for the separation of the parties. Under No. 3, the expressions may include a wide range of actions, and much was left to the discretion of the judge. Here, if anywhere in the law, must come in malicious desertion under the head of cruelties or grave injuries.

In a second chapter, the law treats of the forms of divorce for a determinate cause; of the provisory measures to which the suit for divorce for a determinate cause can give rise ; and of the pleas in bar of action in such cases. The provisions are careful and minute, such as to guard against any improper haste or advantage of the complaining party. We cite only one or two particulars from this chapter. The demandant of the divorce must always appear in person through the stages of the cause, and with counsel if he wishes; but his counsel cannot supply his place. When the plea for divorce is based on outrages, etc. (No. 3, above), the judges are not permitted, although the case may be clear, to decree the divorce directly. The woman is authorized to quit her husband's company, and entitled during the interval, until the case be decided, to receive alimony from him, if she have not herself sources of supply for her wants. Then, after a year of "trial" (épreuve), if they are not reunited, the original demandant can make a new citation of the other consort, and the case can go on. When the case has passed onward to its final stage, the demandant is obliged to present himself before the civil officer, for the purpose of having the divorce pronounced, having summoned the other party for that purpose. This must take place within two months after the final judgment, and if such party neglects to have the other summoned, the proceedings are to go for nothing, and he cannot bring a suit for divorce again except on some new ground. Other articles allow the woman, in all causes where specific grounds for divorce are alleged, to quit her husband's domicil for another indicated by the judge, and to receive alimony proportionate to his means, until the case is settled.

Some of the provisions of the chapter on divorce by mutual consent are worthy of note, as showing the anxiety of the redactors of the law lest this principle should multiply divorces greatly. No mutual consent should have any force unless the husband were over twenty-five and the wife at least twenty-one, and under forty-five years of age; unless they had lived together two years, and had not lived together twenty; and unless their mutual consent were authorized by their fathers and mothers, or by other living ascendants according to the rules prescribed in the law concerning marriage.* Then the parties are required to reduce to writing their proposed arrangements in regard to alimony and the guardianship of the children, and to present themselves before the judicial officer of their *arrondissement* together and in person, in order to make before two notaries a declaration of their will. After the judge shall have made to them such representations and exhortations as he shall think fit, and shall have read the fourth chapter of the law relating to the effects of divorce, if

* That is, if no father and mother can give their consent, a grandfather and grandmother must do it, or if they, being of the same line, disagree, the grandfather's consent is enough. Code Civ. §§ 145–150.

they persist in their resolution, they are required to produce before him an inventory of their goods, their arrangements already spoken of, certificates of their birth and marriage, of the birth and death of all the children born of their union, and of the consent of the proper relative in the ascending line to their divorce. A procès-verbal is to be drawn up, into which all these acts are introduced, with a notice to the wife to reside in a house agreed upon, apart from her husband, until the case be finished. The declaration of the parties touching their mutual consent shall be renewed with the same formalities in the first half of the fourth, seventh, and tenth month after the first proceedings, at which times formal proof must be adduced that their relatives continue to give their assent. At the expiration of a year from their original declaration they are required to appear, supported each by two friends of fifty years old and upward, before the judicial officer of the arrondissement, in order to present to him the acts drawn up on the four occasions already mentioned, and to demand of him separately, yet in the presence of each other and of the four friends, a decree of divorce. Then the reports of all the proceedings hitherto are to be submitted to the "*ministère public*," who, if he finds all the formalities of the law complied with, shall give his conclusions in the form "*la loi permet*," and shall refer the matter to "the tribunal." If the tribunal is of opinion that the parties have satisfied the law, it shall allow the divorce and send the parties to the civil officer in order to have it pronounced; otherwise the tribunal shall declare that the divorce cannot take place, and shall draw up the reasons for such a conclusion. The parties are to appear before the officer authorized to pronounce the divorce within twenty days after the decree of the tribunal, failing to do which they render the decree of the tribunal without effect.*

The next chapter on the effects of divorce will show more clearly still, by several of its provisions, the intention, already made apparent, of putting as many clogs on divorce by mutual consent as possible. This chapter prescribes that divorced parties shall never marry each other again; that when the divorce is for a determinate cause, ten months must elapse before the woman can contract a second marriage; that the guilty partner, where adultery is the cause of divorce, can never

* These provisions of the Code Civil were reproduced in a Rheinische Gesetzbuch, a code founded on the Code Civil, we believe, and controlling a part of the Rhenish provinces of Prussia. That divorce by mutual consent is there unfrequent is shown by the fact which Savigny mentions, that in thirty-six years only seventeen such divorces took place in a population of more than two millions, of whom about a fifth belonged to the Evangelical Church, (Reform of the laws on divorce, u. s., v. 282). Probably, however, the Catholic habits of a good part of this population ought to be taken into consideration in explaining this fact, and to this Savigny does not advert.

marry his or her accomplice; and that the woman, if an adulteress, shall be shut up in a house of correction for not less than three months, nor more than two years. When the divorce is by mutual consent, the parties cannot marry again during three years after the pronunciation of the divorce, and half of the property of each of them, from the day of their first declaration of their purpose to procure a divorce, shall be transferred to the offspring of their marriage in full right—they themselves having the enjoyment of the property during the minority of the children, subject, however, to the proper charges for the children's maintenance and education. In all other kinds of divorce, except for mutual consent, the party against whom the divorce has been obtained shall lose all advantages conceded by the other consort, whether by contract of marriage, or since its consummation; while, on the other hand, the party who has obtained the divorce (the innocent party) shall continue to enjoy the advantages conceded by the other party, whether originally reciprocal or not. Power, also, is given to the courts to grant to such innocent party, if not already having the means of support, an alimony from the revenues of the other party, not exceeding a third part of them, and revocable when no longer needed. Of the arrangements in relation to the children, we omit to speak.

The last chapter of this divorce law relates to separation, "*de corps*," or *a mensa et toro*. This cannot originate in mutual consent, but only in some determinate ground. If it is obtained on account of the adultery of the wife, she shall be shut up in a house of correction for the term already mentioned, but the husband may terminate the effect of this penalty by consenting to take her back again before it has expired. A separation for any other cause except a wife's adultery, after it has lasted three years, may be converted into divorce by a court on the demand of the party who was originally the defendant, provided the original demandant does not consent to put an end to the separation at once.

Here, as we have said, the authors of the law went back upon Catholic principles, which knew no other separation of a married pair, and never dissolved marriage; it agrees, again, with the old ecclesiastical usage in shutting up for a time the woman guilty of adultery, and it thus contemplates, as the church did, a reconciliation; but its peculiarity consists in converting the separation into full divorce after a term of years. There must be a limit of time after which the party sinned against in the first instance shall decide whether he or she will receive back the other, or shall put it into the other's power to marry some other person. The law, although it runs athwart of the Catholic doctrine of the indissolubility of marriage, yet does no hurt to tender Catholic consciences. For the divorce on petition of the original defendant—who might be a Protestant or of no religion —while it allows the other party to marry, does not force him or her to swerve from the strictest principles of his religion. It only says that he shall not by his bitterness of spirit put an obstacle in the way both of reconciliation and of the other party's remarriage, except in the case of his wife's adultery, when his refusal to take her back can make the separation perpetual. The guilty woman might thus be placed on worse ground by this process of separation than by divorce, for the law lays no impediment in the way of her remarriage after divorce when her time of imprisonment is served out, except that of marrying the partner of her crime. In the draft of the chapter on the effects of divorce submitted to the council of state, it was provided that the adulterous woman could never marry again, but on the remark of M. Tronchet, that this prohibition would have a dangerous influence on morals by furnishing an excuse for the lewdness of such a woman, the clause was struck out.

This law of divorce continued in force until the fall of Napoleon, when with the Bourbons the old order of things was restored. It was natural, or rather necessary, that an attempt should now be made to alter the law by abolishing divorce altogether. Of this important change the excellent historian of the restoration, Louis de Viel-Castel, thus speaks (Hist. de la Restauration, iv., 486.):

"The only proposition which did not meet with

serious opposition was that which had for its aim the abolition of divorce. On this point the Assembly was unanimous, and it represented, if not the unanimity, at least the general sentiment of France. M. Trinquelague, the organ of the committee to which the examination of the question had been referred, developed, in a carefully written report ideas similar to those set forth by M. Bonald. He showed that the proposition made no attack on the religious liberty of the Protestants, since, if their religion permitted, it did not prescribe divorce. He indicated the arrangements to be made in order to remedy by legal separation some of the inconveniences which the authors of the Code Civil thought they saw in the indissolubility of marriage, and thus to determine in case of separation the condition of wives and children. The project of a resolution, voted without being opposed, was sent to the Chamber of Peers. Two bishops spoke there in its support. Another member, although he adhered to its principle and made no formal amendment, asked whether divorce could not be allowed to non-catholics for determinate causes, but that idea was set aside, and the resolution was adopted by one hundred and thirteen votes against eight. Transmitted then to the government, and by it reduced to the project of a law, it was definitively sanctioned by the two chambers. The majority in the Chamber of Deputies was two hundred and twenty-five against eleven. In the hurry of accomplishing what was regarded as a work of moral reparation, time enough was not taken for regulating all the difficulties to which separation substituted for divorce would give rise."

In 1830 an attempt was made without success to alter the law of divorce. Of this A. L. Von Rochau thus writes (Gesch. Frankreichs von 1814 bis 1852, 1, 329). : "Some other projects of law, accepted in the Chamber of Deputies, met in the Chamber of Peers with unexpected opposition. The first of these propositions aimed at the reintroduction of divorce, which, under the Restoration, in mockery of sound reason and sound morals, had been unconditionally prohibited in the name of the interests of Christianity, the demoralizing separation from bed and board being put into its place, which leaves behind only the name of marriage, or rather a bald lie." We are not aware of any new attempt to alter the law since the discussions on this project, which were protracted through several years, and ended in the retention —the final retention, says our author writing in 1858—of the prohibition of divorce.

We close the present chapter with a brief sketch of the history of divorce in England.

In the times when England was under the Roman Church, the ecclesiastical courts had cognizance of marriage and its dissolution. No separations except *a mensa et toro* were known.

The same rules in regard to annulment of marriage prevailed, which are still in force in the Catholic countries. The rupture of Henry VIII. with Rome, and the subsequent progress of the Reformation, made no change in the law of marriage and in the courts to which its execution was confided. Catharine of Aragon was set aside by sentence of an ecclesiastical court, because her relation of sister-in-law to the king was claimed to have rendered their marriage null *ab initio*. Anne of Cleves was put away after betrothal, but without consummation of marriage as it is alleged, on the ground of precontract. Anne Boleyn and Catharine Howard were executed for treason, the treason consisting in adultery, which dishonored the king's person and injured the succession. About the same time, the sister of Henry VIII., Margaret of Scotland, got from Rome a separation from her second husband, the Earl of Angus, on the pretext of a precontract between him and another lady.

There came in, however, with the Reformation and with the denial of the sacramental character of marriage, an opinion that it was right in cases of adultery for the innocent party to marry again. In 1548, Queen Catharine Parr's brother,* the Marquis of Northampton, wished to contract a

* Burnet's History of the Reformation (vol. ii., p. 56 of the 2d folio edition) gives a history of that affair, and an abstract of Cranmer's investigations into the opinions of the fathers. A number of questions were put to learned men, and their answers are given in the collections, No. 20, in the same volume.

second marriage after the decision of the ecclesiastical court separating him from his first wife, a daughter of the Earl of Essex, on account of her elopement or adultery; and a commission was issued to Cranmer and others to inquire into the conformity of such a step with the Scriptures. Cranmer, having largely examined the matter, was inclined to allow remarriage in such a case to an innocent party. A few years after, in 1552, the *reformatio legum ecclesiasticarum*, drawn up principally by Cranmer, and approved by a commission of divines and lawyers, proposed remarriage on the ground of adultery and several other offenses, but did not have the sanction of law, perhaps because the Catholic reaction came on the next year with the accession of Mary.* The Puritans in the church would have favored this change in

* Not having access either to the original edition of this code of canon law published in 1571, under the oversight of Archbishop Parker, nor to the Oxford reprint of 1850, we are compelled to resort to second hands. Lingard says that it allowed divorces on account of adultery, desertion, long absence, cruel treatment, and danger to health and life, and separation without liberty of remarriage on account of incompatibility of temper (iv., chap. v., p. 284). Hallam (Const. Hist., i., p. 140) affirms that Lingard turns *capitates inimicitiæ* into incompatibility, which it certainly is not. The code also punished adultery with imprisonment or transportation for life, and in the case of the offending wife with forfeiture of her jointure and of all advantages which she might have derived from the marriage, while the offending husband was to return to her her dower, adding to it one-half of his fortune. The clergyman guilty of this crime was to lose his benefice and his estate.

the laws both then and afterward. Meanwhile, Northampton, having actually taken a second wife, was at first parted from her, then was allowed by sentence of a court to live with her, and finally had his union legalized by act of Parliament. From this time on, we believe, the received doctrine was that a sentence of an ecclesiastical court could only separate from bed and board, and that a special act of Parliament was needed to authorize remarriage.

But for a number of years, although remarriage after divorce was null and void, so that the issue would not be legitimate, no civil penalties were attached to it, and it was punishable only by ecclesiastical censures. Accordingly, many without scruple married again after obtaining divorce in the reign of Elizabeth. In the first year of James a statute made remarrying, while a former husband or wife was living, a felony, and yet a provision of this act declared that it was not to extend to any, who, at the time of such remarriage, had been or should be divorced by sentence of an ecclesiastical court. At the same time several canons touching this matter were enacted by royal authority, one of which provided that no persons separated *a toro et mensa* should, during their joint lives, contract matrimony with other persons, and that the parties requiring the sentence

Hallam thinks that it was laid aside because public feeling was against it.

of divorce should give sufficient caution and security into the court that they would not transgress this restraint. Another canon required the judge who should grant divorce, without observing these rules, to be suspended for one year by the archbishop or bishop, and declared his sentence utterly void.*

A very remarkable case of remarriage, in defiance of these laws, occurred in 1605, between Penelope Devereux, Lady Rich, and the Earl of Devonshire, before known as Lord Montjoy. She had had an adulterous connection with Montjoy, and had borne him several children while the lawful wife of Lord Rich. Then, by an amicable arrangement between the parties, an ecclesiastical court separated her from her husband, and she immediately married her paramour. William Laud, then the Earl's chaplain, solemnized the marriage. Laud must have done this against his own convictions of duty, and he kept the day as a time of fasting afterward.†

The special acts of Parliament enabling a party to marry again, while a former husband or wife was living, were generally preceded by the decree of an ecclesiastical court, but this was not always

* See "The Romance of the Peerage," by Prof. Craik, vol. i., Appendix, which rectifies several mistakes on this matter, and from which we have drawn freely. For the case of Lady Rich and the Earl of Devonshire, see the same work, vol. i., 273. The same work notices the absurd plea made for Laud by Heylyn.

† For Foljambe's case see note on Chapter 4, in the Appendix.

the case. The Duke of Norfolk, without any such prejudgment in Doctors' Commons, was, in 1700, by act of Parliament, after evidence had been submitted, released from all connection with his wife, having vainly endeavored to effect the same thing eight years before, when his case seems to have been made a party question. This adulterous wife, after the dissolution of marriage, was married to her paramour. There had been but one act before this enabling an innocent husband to marry again. The case was that of Lord Ross or Roos, afterward Earl and Duke of Rutland. Here the sentence of the ecclesiastical court had preceded the divorce by act, the proceedings on which, begun in 1666, were not dispatched until four years afterward. Bishop Cosin seems to have aided the passage of this act by several speeches in the House of Lords, the substance of which is given in the State Trials.*

It may be added that the House of Lords, in trials before it, has not necessarily respected the decisions of the ecclesiastical court. In the noted trial of the Duchess of Kingston in 1770, she was found guilty of bigamy, after her marriage to the duke wearing that title. This decision of the Lords invalidated or overrode a decree of an ecclesiastical court, which, in a process of jactitation

* Vol. xiii., pp. 1332–1338, where the proceedings in the Duke of Norfolk's case are given on his last attempt to get an act for his divorce. The proceedings in 1692 are found in vol. xii.

of marriage, had long before restrained Augustus John Hervey, afterward Earl of Bristol, from giving himself out as her husband; for only on the fact of a marriage with him her bigamy depended. And in truth the decrees of the ecclesiastical courts, being often made on mere *ex parte* evidence, or procured by collusion, were deserving of no great respect.

For a long time the Parliament was called on merely to declare children born of an adulteress illegitimate,* or far more frequently to dissolve marriage on account of a decision in the court; until in 1857 the law was remodeled and the jurisdiction in cases of divorce was changed. The law is quoted as 20 and 21 Vict., cap. 85, and was amended, but not essentially, in 1858 and 1860 (21 and 22 Vict., cap. 108, and 23 and 24 Vict., cap. 144). We have these laws before us, and their leading provisions in regard to divorce are as follows:

1. All jurisdiction of ecclesiastical courts in regard to matters matrimonial is henceforth to cease, except so far as relates to marriage licenses, and a new court is created, consisting of the Lord Chancellor, the Chief Judge, and Senior Puisne Judge of the three Common Law Courts, and the

* A case of an early date, where the injured husband asked only this, is mentioned in State Trials, xiii., 1348. Also Lord Ross got such an act, before he obtained the other dissolving his marriage.—Ibid.

Judge of her Majesty's Court of Probate. Three or more of these judges, of whom the Probate Judge is to be one, shall hear and determine all petitions for the dissolution of marriage, and applications for new trials of questions or issues before a jury. This court is to be called the court for divorce and matrimonial causes.

2. A sentence of judicial separation, superseding but equivalent to the former divorce *a mensa et toro*, may be obtained by husband or wife on the ground of adultery, or cruelty, or desertion without cause, for two years and upward. Then follow provisions in regard to the way of obtaining such a sentence; to the court, its rules and principles, which are to conform to those of the ecclesiastical courts; to the alimony of the wife, and her status during separation; to the reversal of a sentence obtained during the absence of the other party, etc.

3. Dissolution of marriage may be obtained by the husband for the adultery of his wife, and by the wife not for simple adultery, but for "incestuous adultery, bigamy with adultery, rape, sodomy or bestiality, or for adultery coupled with such cruelty as without adultery would have entitled the wife to a divorce *a mensa et toro*, or for adultery coupled with desertion without reasonable excuse for two years and upward."* The case is

* Incestuous adultery is defined in the act to mean "adultery with a woman with whom, if his wife were dead, the husband

to come before the court on petition of the innocent party, with statement of facts; the alleged adulterer is to be a correspondent to the petition, if presented by the husband, and the alleged partaker of the husband's crime is to be made a respondent to the petition, if presented by the wife, unless in such case the court order otherwise. If the facts are contested, either party may have a right to a jury-trial.

4. The court being satisfied of the facts, and that there has been no condonation, collusion, or connivance at the crime on the part of the petitioner, and no collusion with a respondent, shall decree a dissolution of the marriage. But the court shall be under no obligation to pronounce such a decree, if it finds that the petitioner himself or herself has been guilty of adultery during the marriage, or of unreasonable delay in presenting the petition, or of cruelty, or of desertion before the adultery, or of misconduct conducing to such crime.

5. Appeal may be made from the Judge Ordinary to a full court, and from such court to the House of Lords, each within three months, unless the recess of the house make a short extension of the term for the final appeal necessary. When no

could not lawfully contract marriage, by reason of her being within the prohibited degrees of consanguinity or affinity." Bigamy is marriage to any other person during the life of the former husband or wife, wherever that marriage shall have taken place.

appeal is made within the prescribed term, or, if made, effects no change in the original decree, the parties may marry again, that is the innocent and the adulterous party both; but no clergyman of the Church of England and Ireland shall be compelled to solemnize the marriage of persons so divorced.

6. Several other provisions of the act are worthy of mention. We have room only for the following: The old action of a husband for criminal conversation is declared to be no longer maintainable, but the husband may claim damages from the alleged adulterer, and the damages, or a part of the damages recovered by verdict of a jury, may be applied by the court for the benefit of the children of the marriage, or for the maintenance of the wife. When such an adulterer shall have been made a co-respondent, and the guilt shall have been established, the court may make him pay the whole or any part of the costs. When the wife is the guilty party and is entitled to property in possession or in reversion, the court, at its discretion, may settle such property or any part of it on the innocent party or on the children of the marriage.

This law it will be observed, grants separation for a small number of specific acts, and dissolution of marriage for all adultery of the wife, but only for adultery attended with aggravating circumstances on the part of the husband. In cases of separation it allows the possibility of renewed cohabitation by mutual agreement, although of this nothing, we believe, is said. In cases of dissolution of marriage it allows both parties to marry again at once, and the guilty one to marry his or her paramour, putting a premium thus on adultery, unless the injured party is determined not to sue for a divorce. In allowing the court to settle a guilty wife's property on her husband or children, it approaches a principle of the Roman law concerning dower. But it falls below the Roman law in making adultery no civil crime, but only a private injury. It respects the consciences of clergymen in not requiring them to solemnize marriages regarded by them as unlawful. On the whole, with serious defects, it seems to us to be an excellent law; it does honor to the Christian country where it is in force, and it is certainly a great improvement on the former mode of regulating divorce in England. May the door never open wider in England for the more censurable kinds of divorce, nor the sanctities of domestic life lose that reverence which they now possess!

CHAPTER V.

DIVORCE AND DIVORCE LAWS IN THE UNITED STATES.

We propose, in the present chapter, to give some account of the state of divorce in our own country. A full view of this subject would embrace the law of divorce, the procedure of the courts in such cases, and the statistics of the subject. The last head ought to include the number of applications granted, the causes for which they were granted, and and the number refused. In this broad field the materials are either too many or too few, or lie outside of our appropriate province. The law of divorce must be gathered from the statutes of a great number of independent law-making bodies, which are not unfrequently changing their legislation, so that supplement after supplement must be consulted to find out what is the last wisdom of the representatives of the people. The procedure of the courts belongs chiefly to the domains of lawyers, and is of use in our investigations only so far as it affects the facility of obtaining divorce and opens a temptation to discontented husbands or wives. The statistics are meagre; there are none known to us of the number of rejected petitions save in a single instance; and few of the States have published tables of the applications granted. The great State of New York, for instance, still allows this information to lie buried in the offices of the clerks of sixty counties. It will not be strange then, especially as statistical science is as yet new and imperfect in this country, if our exhibition of this part of the subject, although presenting some important results, shall be judged to be unsatisfactory. It is so to ourselves, and we regard this essay rather as breaking a path for others, than as having in itself a permanent value. May we not hope that some member of the new and vigorous society of Social Science will take up this subject and bring to light something more complete.

The first point to which we call attention, is the divorce laws of the several States of the Union. Here to avoid endless repetition we shall endeavor to bring the necessary details under a few heads, not feeling ourselves bound to do more than to give examples from classes of States, so far as they can be classified. No such details are furnished to us from others, except the scanty ones in the notes to Chancellor Kent's 27th lecture (vol. 2, 95–128). Mr. Bishop, in his standard work on marriage and divorce (4th ed., 1864), declines setting out "*in extenso* the statute laws of our several States, relating to marriage or relating to divorce. Should this be done," says he, "a great number of our pages would be occupied with the work, while very little benefit indeed would result to the reader. But it is observable," he continues, "that the statutory law of this country, relating to this subject, seems in general to have been drawn up by men who either did not possess much knowledge of the unwritten law which governs it, or did not regard such unwritten law as worthy to be considered by them in framing the statutes; and who, moreover, gave but little thought to the matter of the practical working of the statutes. The interpretations of these enactments, therefore, becomes a subject of great difficulty." One of his proofs of the truth of these remarks is taken from the general statutes of his own State, Massachusetts, where there is a provision (chap. 107, § 6), that a divorce from the bond of matrimony may be decreed for *adultery* or *impotency* of either party. But impotency, to justify divorce, must be according to common law an impediment at the commencement of marriage, rendering it voidable but not void, while adultery anterior to marriage is no cause of divorce at all. And again a sentence of divorce on the former ground declares that the marriage was originally void, but one on the latter assumes that the marriage was originally valid. Here there is a jumbling together of causes annulling and causes dissolving marriage; and the same is true of the laws of many of the other States which speak of impotency barely, while other laws are careful to define it as existing before marriage. How could such a provision be interpreted without a knowledge of common law? For under some codes *impotentia superveniens* may dissolve marriage, and more frequently a previous adultery renders remarriage unlawful, or at least unlawful during the life of the innocent party.

Coming now to the laws of the several States we shall find that in some of the oldest ones their origin has had important influence on legislation down to the present time. The Puritans brought English law with them, but separated from it in the matter of divorce, by following, as they supposed, the rules of the New Testament. Adultery and desertion were thus the only causes of divorce, and from this beginning their legislation, following the analogy between desertion and certain other kindred offenses, degenerated until it lost sight of the New Testament entirely. Other colonies adhered more nearly to English law, or, as Maryland, may have been influenced by the Roman Catholic doctrine of marriage and so confined divorce within narrower limits. Louisiana has been subject to varying forces in the transition from a dependency of France and Spain to the complete American character. In the newer

States various concurrent influences may have shaped the divorce laws, such as the views of some prominent man among the earlier settlers, and the origin, foreign or domestic, of large classes of their inhabitants.

At first divorces were mainly, if not exclusively, granted by an act of a colonial legislature in accordance with the practice then and until recently existing in England. In the "general laws and liberties of the Massachusetts colony" printed in 1672, there is no mention made of divorce. In the laws published in 1699, the only provision we find in relation to divorce is that all controversies concerning marriage and divorce shall be heard and determined by the Governor and Council. Kent states in regard to more recent times, that the constitutions of Georgia, Alabama, and Mississippi allowed divorce only by vote of two-thirds of each branch of the legislature after trial and verdict of a superior court, or a court of chancery. But later constitutions have, in all these States, rendered such actions of the law-making body unnecessary, if not forbidden its exercise altogether. He adds that in Maryland, Virginia, and South Carolina, the legislature and not the courts had power to decree divorce. In Connecticut and New York, where the courts had jurisdiction, it was not exclusive, but the legislatures of these States occasionally made use of this power down to 1839–1840. "In 1836 divorces *a vinculo* were granted by the legislature of Illinois, without any cause assigned, and in 1837 by that of Missouri." But the evils and the questionable right of such special legislation have in great measure put an end to it. Such special legislation is now prohibited by the constitutions of at least twenty-three of the States, among the rest by that of New York framed in 1846; and almost all the recent constitutions contain similar restrictions.* Yet this way of granting divorces has not wholly disappeared. In 1865 an act of the *loyal* body then claiming to represent Virginia divorced a woman in Norfolk County from her husband; the same thing took place in Maine last year (1867); Pennsylvania still adheres to such legislation, within the limits of a constitutional provision "that the legislature shall not have power to enact laws annulling the contract of marriage, in any case where by law the courts of the commonwealth are, or may be hereafter, empowered to grant divorce;" and while we write there is a petition before the General Assembly of Connecticut, to dissolve marriage in a case not included within the general statute. Such acts have occupied the ground as well of sentences of nullity as

*New York (const. of '46), N. Jersey ('44), Maryland ('57), West Virginia ('61-3), Florida ('65), Alabama (?), Mississippi (32), Louisiana ('64), Tennessee ('39-66), Texas ('66), Michigan ('50), Minnesota ('57-58), Wisconsin ('48), Indiana ('51), Illinois ('47-48), Iowa ('57), Missouri ('65), Kentucky ('50), Kansas ('59), Nebraska ('67), Nevada ('64), California ('49), Oregon ('57).

of divorce proper and of separation from bed and board. This is a broader field than the English parliament went over in their special acts of divorce legislation, which never provided for any other dissolution of marriage than the absolute one. And yet in England the occasion for this kind of legislative intervention was greater, and the power to exercise it clearer. It has been contended that such acts violate the Constitution of the United States by impairing the obligation of contracts, that they are retrospective, and that they confound the functions of the law-maker with those of the judge. But if they merely declare a contract broken, they do not impair the obligation of contracts nor take the shape of *ex post facto* legislation; and if they are confined to cases of an extraordinary character, where the courts could not well provide a remedy, they involve no confusion of governmental functions. Still they are on more than one account undesirable.*

The States of the Union, if looked at with reference to their divorce laws, may be divided into those which provide both for absolute divorce and for separation from bed and board, and those which know nothing of the last-mentioned proce-

* Chancellor Kent, Mr. Bishop, and others hold the doctrine here given. Mr. Bishop (vol. 1, § 690) teaches that while such acts are constitutional for the main act of divorcing, they can include no collateral matter, such as a direction for the payment of alimony.

dure. They may also be loosely divided into those which have more closely followed English law, and those which have multiplied the causes of divorce without any precedent drawn from the fatherland, if they did not long ago start from a standing point which was not English. Some influence on legislation in certain States may be due to Scotch law, which grants divorce in cases of desertion, and some perhaps to the laws of Germany. Louisiana has a position of its own, as showing a marked influence of French law, which is shaped to suit its peculiar condition.

We have examined the statutes of about twenty-three States, including nearly all the older ones, and in sixteen of these both absolute and qualified divorces are now authorized. The States which know nothing of separation from bed and board, such as Connecticut, Ohio, S. Carolina, Indiana, and, if we are not in error, Illinois and Missouri, represent the earlier usage of the older colonies. This separation by the civil code of Louisiana (ed. of 1857) is necessary as a forerunner of divorce proper, in all cases except where adultery or sentence of infamous punishment is the ground for the petition to the court. In some States separation from bed and board may be pronounced by decree of court temporary or perpetual; it may be revoked by a formal judicial act; it is generally confined to certain crimes, such as cruelty or drunkenness, or neglect to maintain a wife; but in other States, such as Rhode Island and Kentucky, it can be granted for any crime which is a cause of divorce *a vinculo*, if the parties desire it and the court think fit, and for other causes according to the court's discretion. It may also be followed in some States by divorce *a vinculo*, if the parties are not reconciled within a certain period, as five or ten years. These separations, on the whole, must form a small part of the entire number annually granted: in Massachusetts they constituted, between 1861 and 1865, about one-fourteenth of all the divorces, and they grow in great measure out of the misconduct of husbands. Of course the laws make provision for the support of wives and children in such cases, but in some States, as New York, Ohio, and North Carolina, alimony can also be allowed to a wife without a legal separation. The laws of the last-named State authorize the courts to decree divorce or separation from bed and board, or alimony if no more be demanded, whenever any just cause of divorce exists, thus constituting a third grade of release from married society as one *de facto*, without bringing it into the forms of jural separation.*

We proceed now to give a sketch of the leading provisions of legislation in this country with regard to divorce in general, beginning with those States which have kept closest to the English

* See Bishop, Book V., Chap. 30 and 31.

usage. Here South Carolina may stand at the head, a State in which no case of divorce ever came before the courts, and no divorce was ever granted by the legislature, and which, having had with its old established church no ecclesiastical courts, never granted separation from bed and board. This state of things has continued until the present time. The new constitution, now before Congress for its approval, ordains that "divorces from the bond of matrimony shall not be allowed but by the judgment of a court, as shall be prescribed by law." As the structure of society has undergone a vast change since the outbreak of the rebellion, the State will ere long probably differ but little in its legislation from its neighboring sisters. The causes of the past attitude of South Carolina in regard to divorce have been the original form of civil government, the old established church, and State pride, which long manifested itself in unwillingness to follow the lead of others, rather than any strong religious feeling or regard for the supposed doctrines of the New Testament. As a slave State it has winked at concubinage, and the white wife has often had to endure the infidelity of her husband, as something inevitable, which no law could remedy, and which public opinion did not severely rebuke. "Not only is adultery not indictable there," says Mr. Bishop, "but the legislature has found it necessary to regulate by statute how large a proportion a married man may give of his property to his concubine" (i. § 38). From the same author we quote the following words of Judge Watts, of the State Court, delivered from the bench, showing that the jurists do not regard the system as wholly good, and as deserving of all the boasts which have been spent upon it. "In this country, where divorces are not allowed for any cause whatever, we sometimes see men of excellent characters unfortunate in their marriages, and virtuous women abandoned or driven away houseless by their husbands, who would be doomed to celibacy and solitude, if they did not form connections which the law does not allow, and who make excellent husbands and virtuous wives still." Here the law of 1 James I., making marriage, while a wife or husband is living, felony, which was adopted and inserted among the old laws of the colony, is practically disregarded. Probably this State has been freer than many northern ones from those offenses against the laws of marriage in which the wife is a guilty party, for the reason that the pistol or the dagger can work out its own justice; but there has, beyond question, been a plentiful crop of those other offenses on the part of married men, in which persons of the inferior race have been partakers and victims.

New York is another of the States which has adhered somewhat closely to English law in regard to marriage and divorce. Whether before the transfer of New Netherlands by the peace of Breda from the Dutch to the English in 1671, the Dutch law, allowing divorce for adultery and desertion, was put in practice, we are unable to say, but from that time until the revolution no divorce was granted in the colony, which had now come under English law and the influence of the English Church. For a dozen years from the declaration of independence the legislature of the State had alone the power, after the manner of the parliament of England, to dissolve the marriage tie by an act of special legislation. In 1787 a law was passed authorizing the chancellor to declare marriage dissolved, but only in cases of adultery. Afterward divorces from bed and board were introduced: we find them mentioned in the laws of the State published in 1813. The legislature still intervened by special acts, but this power was taken away by the third State constitution framed in 1846. Amid the changes in the laws and in the courts of this State, the law of divorce and the procedure for dissolving the marriage tie has continued with very little alteration until the present time. Meanwhile English law has been essentially altered, but the changes have brought it into near resemblance to the law of New York in almost all essential features. Both still treat adultery as furnishing ground for private action only. But the New York law has a decided advantage in the way of protecting public morals over the English, as it prohibits the defendant found guilty of adultery from marrying during the life-time of the innocent complaining party.

Chancellor Kent has given us in his lucid and attractive way an exposition of the law and procedure in cases of divorce, as they came before the Court of Chancery, where he so ably presided.* We borrow from him and from the revised statutes (5th ed.) those particulars which it seems important for our purpose to mention. 1. If the offense of adultery is denied there must be a jury trial; if the defendant suffers the bill to be taken *pro confesso*, a referee must be appointed by the court, and the cause must be heard on the proof taken by him and on his report. 2. If the parties were married out of the State, it must be made to appear that they were inhabitants of the State at the time of the commission of the adultery, or that the commission took place within the State, and that the injured party was an inhabitant when the complaint was brought. If the parties were married within the State, it must appear that the complainant was domiciled in the State at the time of the offense and of bringing the suit. Other particulars, such as the actions of the complainant which may be a bar in the way of the petition being granted, and the effect of the divorce on dower

* He died in 1847, shortly after the Court of Chancery, as distinct from the common law courts, ceased, according to the constitution of 1846, to have existence

and on the husband's right in his wife's estate, reappear in the laws of many other states and need no especial mention.

The causes for which divorce from bed and board may be granted are cruelty toward the wife, conduct rendering it unsafe for her to live with the husband, desertion, willful desertion and refusal to make provision for her support. The complaints of the wife must be specific, and may be dismissed if the defendant can bring forward her ill conduct in justification so as to satisfy the court.* If the court separates the parties, it may provide for the support of the wife and children out of the husband's estate, and even if no decree of separation be made, such order for the wife's support may be passed. The decree may be perpetual or for a time, and may be revoked by the court on joint application of the parties upon evidence of reconciliation.

The other States, which seem to have followed English—or it may be Catholic—views of divorce, such as Maryland and Virginia, do not now differ essentially from the mass of their sister States; we pass them by therefore to say a word in regard to the state of divorce in Louisiana, as it is laid down in the civil code (edition of 1857). The code de-

* The husband may sue for divorce on the ground of the wife's cruelty, but the New York revised statutes of 1830 gave this remedy to the wife alone. But as the statute was not repealed, it has been held to remain in force. Bishop, i., § 761.

clares that "the law considers marriage in no other light than as a civil contract," meaning by this we suppose that it has nothing to do with the moral and religious aspects of the institution. But when it goes on to say that marriage is a contract intended at its origin to endure until the death of the contracting parties, it seems a little inconsistent with itself, for whence can this indissolubility be derived but from moral and religious considerations. If the law will regard nothing to be marriage but such a permanent relation, it must be because concubinage for a time, although agreed to by contract between the parties, has an immoral character. The law itself has these peculiarities, that any offense for which divorce may be granted, may also be the cause of separation from bed and board; and that for every offense, excepting two, this separation must precede divorce proper by a certain length of time. These two causes of immediate divorce are adultery and sentence of infamous punishment; and by adultery in the case of the husband is intended, as in the French code, his keeping a concubine in the house, or openly and publicly elsewhere. In other cases two years must have elapsed, since the sentence of separation without reconciliation of the parties, before divorce can be granted. The remaining causes of separation mentioned in the code are cruel conduct, making life insupportable, abandonment, defamation, and attempt of either party on the life of the other.

A statute of 1827 ordains that no divorce shall be granted except for adultery, infamous punishment, cruel conduct as above, and abandonment for five years, in which case a summons to return to the common dwelling must be made one year before application for the divorce. Are we then to understand that defamation and attempt on life can separate for a time, but not dissolve the marriage tie? As for the party guilty of adultery, it is provided that he or she can never marry the partner in crime, without incurring the penalty of bigamy, and having the marriage pronounced null.

We pass now to the laws of the great majority of the States, the leading characteristics of which are to grant divorce, or it may be separation, for a great variety of offenses, to take no account of religious considerations, and thus to aim at removing difficulties, which arise between partners in marriage, in a way which is revolting to the mass of Christian people. Add to this, to a considerable extent, a great looseness of procedure, which, in the extreme instances of it, opens the door to greater evils than the laws themselves, if severely applied, would produce.

These laws furthermore do not fairly represent the original plan of colonial legislation. The older States have in the course of time fallen far below the strictness of their ancient laws, and the new have started from the lower position on a downward road. It was natural for Maryland at first to be under the influence of the Catholic doctrine of divorce, and for Virginia to follow the model of England. The Puritan colonies began their legislation with two causes for divorce, adultery and desertion, holding in common with their Scotch and Dutch brethren, and indeed with the Reformed Churches generally, as well as with the Lutheran, that the New Testament recognizes both of these as sufficient grounds for the dissolution of marriage. Desertion at that time was a very different thing from that which it is now. To go to some remote colony, or to the West Indies, or to the old country, from disaffection of mind, or with the spirit of a vagabond, implied lifelong severance of family ties, and the probabilities were great that such a step involved adultery also. To these two causes was added absence for seven years in parts unknown without being heard of, which, in a law of the Massachusetts colony passed in the 5th of William and Mary, is modified to suit certain hard cases, into "three years' absence for one gone to sea, the ship not being heard of for three years, when a voyage is usually made in three months." But this is not really a third cause of divorce; it is only a declaration that the probabilities of death were so strong that a new marriage after that lapse of time ought not to be regarded as bigamy. And, indeed, a law of the first year of James the First, which lays down this same principle, and fixes on this very term of years in applying it, must have furnished a model and an authority to the colonists. Such was the early legislation, which continued substantially unaltered until after the revolution shook and broke off the old traditions, and a new development of society began. When now marriage came to be looked upon more and more as a mere contract, when religious and moral considerations were kept apart from political, when legislation, perhaps in inexperienced hands, set about removing palpable evils without looking at remote consequences, when cities with their peculiar vices and their low population grew in size and number, when an emigration from the Eastern States gave up its lands and homes to an inferior class of society, and in the West many of the foreign settlers had been trained up under loose laws of divorce—when such causes as these were acting, it is not strange that laxer principles, touching the sanctity of marriage, crept in and expressed themselves in legislation. But aside from these social causes of change in the laws, we must admit that there was a kind of logical necessity for a broader system of divorce. If desertion was a good ground for divorce, it might be asked why should not neglect to provide for a wife, or refusal of cohabitation be such also, which are kinds of desertion, or imprisonment for crime, which is enforced desertion. Why should not cruelty and intemperance be good grounds, which practically break up the family union? And as there are other actions which lie on the borders of these, why should not they be good grounds for divorce, if the sufferer desires it? And so, for aught we know, by and by, it may be argued that, as the essence of the marriage, considered in its spirit, is love, when this ceases, there is no good reason why marriage should not cease at the pleasure of the parties. Thus we come to the Roman practice, to the conception of marriage as a mere contract, and to the principle that incompatibility of temper or a new passion may legitimately put an end to what even the Roman lawyers called the *individua vitæ consuetudo.*

It would be a dreary and profitless task, if we were able to undertake it, to give even an abstract of the laws relating to divorce of a large number of separate commonwealths. All that we shall attempt is to enumerate the causes, which authorize the dissolution of marriage in any of those States of which we have not already particularly spoken.

1. Adultery. This can be followed by divorce everywhere, and the definition is substantially the same throughout the States. It is, as the statutes of Rhode Island define it, illicit intercourse of two persons, one of whom is married. Certain States, as Alabama and Mississippi, in their criminal laws punish living together in open and notorious or continued adultery rather than a single, act if brought to light; but we suppose

that they would not depart, in the practice of the court, from the ordinary definition of this country. It is a singularity of the laws of one State that the cohabitation of divorced persons subjects them to the penalty for adultery.

2. Desertion. This offense is called by several names, as "abandonment," "utter," "malicious," "wilful and continued," "continued and obstinate" desertion,—"absence without good cause," "abandonment and desertion." The sense in all the forms and expression is no doubt the same. Absence from the common dwelling and the society of the wife or husband, not for the purpose of business, but with the evil or "malicious intent of not fulfilling conjugal obligations," and that absence, not interrupted by occasional visits, but continued long enough to test the disposition of the offender, may be said to constitute the offense thus described in different words. What the time of continued absence shall be is generally indicated in the statutes. In Indiana it is "one year, or less,"* if the court is satisfied that reconciliation is improbable, and in Missouri two years without good cause. In four or five other States it is two years (Pennsylvania, Michigan, Illinois, Alabama, Tennessee), and three years in seven others (Maine, New Hampshire, Vermont, Connecticut, Maryland, Georgia, Mississippi), while

* But by an act of 1859, "or less" and what follows is stricken out.

five years—the prescribed time in Massachusetts, New Jersey, Virginia, and Louisiana—is the maximum fixed in any of our laws. The statutes of Rhode Island prescribe five years or less according to the judge's discretion. In one or two States there is no time specified, as seems to be the case in New York and North Carolina. In a number of these States it is made to involve, if proved, separation from bed and board, in others divorce *a vinculo*, and in one or two the one or the other according to the aggravation of the offense as estimated by the court. In Massachusetts desertion for five consecutive years may furnish cause for separation, and a libel in this case is not defeated by a temporary return of the deserting party, if it seems not to have been *bona fide* but to have proceeded from an intention to defeat the divorce. The wife, leaving the husband on account of extreme cruelty or neglect to maintain her, does not desert him, and has her remedy as an injured party. After separation from bed and board, if no reconciliation take place, the originally innocent party can obtain a divorce at the end of five years, or either party at the end of ten. *

* A curiosity of legislation is the act of Georgia, passed March 18, 1865, just before the Confederacy collapsed, to the effect that divorce *a vinculo*, may be granted to loyal females whose husbands are in the service of the United States, or have been voluntarily within the lines of the enemy, giving them aid and

3. Imprisonment for crime is absence or forced separation, caused by the guilt of one of the parties, and preventing the fulfillment of conjugal and family duties. For this reason, and perhaps on account of the disgrace also, most of the States regard this as cause for divorce or separation. The length and the place of imprisonment and the kind of crime are variously defined. In Massachusetts hard labor for five years or for life is a good ground for divorce, and no pardon has any effect on the sentence. In Maine imprisonment for life dissolves marriage without legal process. Vermont agrees with Massachusetts except in the time of confinement, which is made to be three years or more. In other statutes the punishment authorizing divorce must be infamous, or for felony, or in a penitentiary, and its length two years, or not less than two, or for life.

4. In the statutes of a few States, as New Hampshire, Massachusetts, and Kentucky, joining a religious society which holds marriage to be unlawful—together with refusal to cohabit with the married partner for six months, as the law of New Hampshire adds, in a somewhat ambiguous construction of words—is made a ground for divorce. And accordingly there appears one case of divorce from a wife for this reason in the lists of divorces of Massachusetts during five years.

comfort. Compare what is said of a similar cause of divorce in French law, in Chapter IV.

The law of this State prescribes that the membership in such a sect shall have lasted three years before a libel can be presented, while that of New Hampshire, if we understand it, reduces the time to six months' refusal of cohabitation after joining religionists of this description.

5. Neglect to provide for a wife's maintenance or support lies between desertion and cruelty. So this also is added in a number of statutes as a reason for divorce, or for separation in those codes to which separation is known. This is at one time described as neglect or refusal of the husband to support the wife, when he has the ability (Rhode Island), at another as a wasting of his estate and neglect to provide for his family (Kentucky), or the refusal suitably to maintain a wife (Massachusetts), or gross and wanton neglect to maintain a wife (Michigan), or refusal to provide for her (New York). This wrong of the husband may involve separation in the last-named State, in Maine, and in Massachusetts; separation, or, if the court thinks fit, divorce in Michigan and Rhode Island; and divorce in Kentucky.

6. Connected with neglect to provide for the family and with cruelty also, are habits of intoxication, which are a cause of divorce or more frequently of separation in many of the codes. Sometimes this is described as habitual drunkenness (New Hampshire and other States), sometimes as gross and confirmed habits of drunkenness (Massa-

chusetts), while again we find in some codes a specification of the length of time during which the habit has lasted. It is three years' habitual drunkenness in New Hampshire and two years in Missouri. In North Carolina a statute authorizes the court, if a man becomes a spendthrift or a drunkard, to decree alimony without separation, provided the creditors are not thereby injured.

7. In almost all the statutes which we have consulted, cruelty, under some form of words or other, is a cause for either absolute or qualified divorce. Probably there is no code of any State in which this does not appear. It is described in such phrases as intolerable severity (Vermont), extreme cruelty (New Hampshire, Maine, and other States), cruel and abusive treatment (Massachusetts), intolerable cruelty (Connecticut), cruelty and conduct rendering cohabitation unsafe for the wife (New York); as cruelties endangering life, and indignities making life burdensome (Pennsylvania), which the laws of North Carolina and Tennessee substantially repeat, the first adding to it turning the wife out of doors, the other, ejection. Louisiana has much the same definition. Tennessee further adds in her code attempts on life by poison or other malicious means, which is made a cause of divorce, while cruelties, indignities, and ejection are causes of separation. In Kentucky, the cruelty, or gross cruelty, is measured by the time: it must have continued six

months; but another specification is added—cruel beating or injury—to which no such continuance is attached, so that a single act, for any thing that appears, may be a sufficient cause of divorce.

In some statutes it seems to be assumed that the husband only will be guilty of cruelty, as the stronger party; in others, the expressions are indefinite, and may apply to both. What the view of the courts is on this point may be learned from Mr. Bishop's work (i., §§ 761–763). In the list of divorces granted during five years, published by order of the legislature of Massachusetts, by the side of one hundred and nineteen divorces or separations, granted for cruelty of the husband, there appear three for cruelty of the wife. Taken in a wide sense, as including indignities and conduct rendering life unsafe, the remedy may be as much needed in some cases by the one sex as by the other.

Besides these causes for interference in the relations of married persons, some of the codes introduce others which occurred before the marriage, and rendered the union either void and unlawful altogether, or voidable if the complaining party chooses to assert his or her rights. As these cases have properly nothing to do with our discussion, which is confined within causes for divorce occurring after marriage, and as they are illogically brought together with divorces proper, we may pass them by. We may, however, notice those laws which prohibit marriage between a white and a black person, or between a freeman and a slave, as either now of questionable constitutionality, since the races are placed on an equality, or as no longer having any application.

A few of the States have somewhat remarkable provisions in their divorce laws, which deserve particular attention, either as opening a wide door of divorce or as putting the whole subject within the discretion of the courts. In the Revised Statutes of Maine (1857), after causes for divorce had been mentioned, as if the burden of specifying numerous particulars was quite too great for the law-maker or the codifier, we find it said that divorce *a vinculo* may be granted by any justice of the Supreme Court, at any term, in the county of the residence of either party to the application, "whenever, in the exercise of a sound discretion, he deems it reasonable and proper, conducive to domestic harmony, and consistent with the peace and morality of society—if the parties were married in this State, or cohabited here after marriage." In North Carolina, the statute, after providing for certain special cases, adds, that if "any other just cause of divorce exists," the injured party may obtain divorce *a vinculo* or *a mensa et toro*, at the court's discretion, or a decree of alimony only, if no more be demanded (Revised Statutes of 1855). The law of Indiana provides that divorce may be decreed by circuit courts, on petition of a *bona fide* resident in the county, for certain causes, and then adds, and for any other cause for which the court shall deem it proper that a divorce should be granted. But the action of the Circuit Court can be revised by the Supreme Court (Revised Statutes of 1862). In Iowa, the statute authorizes a divorce when the fact appears "that the parties cannot live together in peace and harmony, and that their welfare requires a separation."* In Rhode Island, divorce may be decreed for sundry causes, "and for any other gross misbehavior and wickedness in either of the parties, repugnant to and in violation of the marriage covenant" (Revised Statutes). And in Connecticut a well-known clause of a statute, passed in 1849, allows divorce for "any such misconduct as permanently destroys the happiness of the petitioner, and defeats the purposes of the conjugal relation." The discretion given by some of the laws in so important a matter must be very embarrassing to the judge, and may result in the most diverse usages, according as he has loose or strict notions of the sacredness of marriage. The looseness of others of these laws will, almost of course, stretch the facility of granting divorce to the extreme limit.

In Illinois, the interpretation of the Supreme Court has taken away from the judges what seems on the face of the statute to be a great latitude of

* Bishop, I., § 832.

discretionary power. Besides the causes for divorce arising after marriage, which are five—adultery, desertion, extreme and repeated cruelty, two years' habitual drunkenness, and conviction of felony or other infamous crime—the statute empowers the courts to hear and determine all causes of divorce not authorized by any law of the State, and to decree a dissolution of the marriage bonds, if judged expedient. But the Supreme Court has decided that the discretion given must be limited to common law cases omitted in the enumeration of the statute, viz.: precontract, and relation by blood or by marriage. Applications on these grounds are rarely made.*

A number of laws determine the time of residence in the State before a party can bring a libel or petition for a divorce, and some others prescribe what effect foreign judgments in certain cases are to have within the jurisdiction of the States concerned. Both these points are of extreme importance, as emigration is so easy, and temporary residence in another State may be used for the purpose of obtaining a divorce not possible in the State where the party had a previous domicil, and to which he expects to return. The States are naturally not willing to have their courts used by foreigners, after a short sojourn, for the purpose of effecting a divorce, and the difficulty of ascertain-

* A lawyer of Chicago, S. B. Perry, Esq., has kindly given me this information.

ing whether due notice has been served upon the adverse party, when he is a non-resident, may oftentimes be very great. And, on the other hand, as divorce is more subject to local law than marriage is, so that by the law of nations no *forum* is obliged to recognize the validity of the divorce law of a different religion or state of manners, it will naturally come to pass that a State of the Union will not feel itself obliged by courtesy to allow a divorce granted in another State to have effect within its territory, from which the parties, being residents, or one of them, had gone abroad for the purpose of obtaining the divorce. But into the details of these matters we do not propose to enter; they come within the province of the courts, and the details into which they run must be learned from extensive treatises built on the decisions of courts, such as Mr. Bishop's commentaries. We only add, that a State like Indiana, whose divorce laws are exceedingly loose, where a year's residence qualifies a person to petition for a divorce, where a case can be tried thirty days after notices are published in a newspaper of the county where the suit is brought, and where divorce fully frees both parties from the marriage contract, opens a wide door as well for *ex parte* suits, where the defendant is ignorant of the proceedings, as for gross collusions, and loses its reputation among its sister States. "Nothing is more common," writes a gentleman of high standing, living in one of the cities of Indiana, "than to form an acquaintance with some respectably appearing gentleman or lady who has come a stranger to our city, and learn soon after that the object of the visit is to remain long enough to apply for a divorce. There is, however," he adds, "a growing public sentiment demanding a change." The acts of 1859 indicate a slight influence of a better feeling. Abandonment is put at one year, the clause "or less, if the court is satisfied that reconciliation is improbable" being omitted. The petitioner must have resided—as was said before—one year in the State; and judgments concerning divorce are opened on behalf of non-residents.

Nor need we here do more than allude to the obstacles put in the way of divorce by the laws of many of the States, when some previous conduct of the petitioner furnishes a good reason for the denial of his petition. Such conduct is—especially if adultery be the alleged cause of the petition—the complainant's or petitioner's similar infidelity, condonation, or indulgence shown in cohabiting with the defendant after knowledge of his or her offense, long delay to notice the offense which is at length brought before the courts, or connivance or collusion of the two parties. The principles that dictate such provisions of law will govern the courts where there are no express statutes of such an import.

More important is it for our special object to consider the results of divorce to the parties, the liabilities or disabilities and the penal consequences, if any, which may follow the offense of the guilty party. Here, first of all, the way in which the different States view the sin of adultery is deserving of notice. Some, as New York and South Carolina, have always followed England in not considering it a subject of criminal punishment, nor have we noticed it among the misdemeanors mentioned in the statutes of Kentucky, of Tennessee, or of Louisiana.* In some other codes the penalty is very small—in Maryland it is a fine of ten dollars; in Virginia, of not less than twenty. In most of the States it is an offense subjecting the parties guilty of it to fine or imprisonment, or both, but the amount varies greatly. The fine generally falls between one hundred and five hundred dollars; the imprisonment runs up from confinement in a common jail of not more than sixty days, as in Georgia, or not exceeding six months as in Missouri and several other States, to a year, which is the maximum in most of the codes, or even to five years, as in Vermont, Maine,

* In Mr. Livingston's code the guilty woman forfeits all matrimonial gains and certain leading civil rights. Her partner in guilt is liable to a fine of between one hundred and two thousand dollars, or to imprisonment not more than six months A husband keeping a concubine is subject to the same fines, and loses the right for a certain time of being a tutor or curator to his children.

and Connecticut. In a few States a repetition of the offense increases the penalty. Alabama imposes in the first instance a fine of not less than one hundred dollars, with imprisonment in a county jail, or confinement with hard labor for not more than half a year, while a renewed offense between the same persons trebles the fine and doubles the imprisonment; and a third transgression is visited with two years' hard labor in the penitentiary. The laws of Illinois, again, which impose on each party a fine of two hundred dollars, or six months' imprisonment for the first offense, double or treble it for successive new ones.

The feeling of the early settlers in some of the older colonies was in striking contrast with the tender treatment which adultery meets with from existing laws in this country. The first laws of Massachusetts made it a capital crime. By the laws published in 1699, persons convicted of adultery were set on the gallows with a rope round their neck, one end of which was cast over the gallows, then they were whipped on their way to the jail, not exceeding forty stripes, and were obliged to have a letter A, two inches long, "of color contrary to their clothes," sewed on the sleeve or back of the outer garment, in open view. And if such persons were found without the mark, they were to be whipped not exceeding fifteen stripes for each neglect to wear it. The Connecticut laws of

1673 required the same brand to be burnt in on the forehead, together with the wearing of a halter and public whipping. In Rhode Island, in 1655, a wife confessing her guilt was sentenced by the General Assembly to pay ten pounds fine and to receive thirty stripes in two installments.* And Vermont, although settled so long afterward, in the original laws follows the older colonies of Massachusetts and of Connecticut in its penalties, which are thirty-nine stripes, or an A branded on the forehead and the same mark on the clothes, with a liability of ten stripes if the convicted person is found without it. In the statutes of 1787, the brand on the forehead is omitted, but the guilty persons are set on the gallows and are to wear the mark on their clothing. So also in Pennsylvania, a law of 1705 exposed such persons to twenty-one lashes or a fine of fifty pounds for the first offense, to the same number of lashes with seven years' hard labor, or a fine of one hundred pounds for the second, and for a third to a repetition of the same penalties, besides the brand with the letter A. In Virginia, again, by the law of 1691, a fine of twenty pounds sterling was imposed for every offense, but if the offender was unable to pay the fine, thirty lashes on the back or three months' imprisonment could take its place. In 1696 the money fine disappears, one thousand pounds of tobacco and a cask, or twenty-five lashes, or two

* Arnold's History of Rhode Island, i., 320.

months' imprisonment being now the penalties. In 1705 the statute omits imprisonment, but retains the tobacco and cask or the twenty-five lashes. Thus the Puritan, the Quaker, and the Royalist colonies agree in the severity with which they punish the crime of adultery. But they agree, also, in softening down their legislation on that point. In Pennsylvania imprisonment for a year, or a fine not to exceed five hundred dollars now expresses the indignation of the community on this point. In Virginia, a fine of not less than twenty dollars seems to be the entire penalty. In Massachusetts, the crime is visited with a mulct of five hundred dollars, or imprisonment in the State prison for three years, or in a jail for not more than two. In Vermont the limits are five years' confinement or a thousand dollars fine; while in Connecticut imprisonment for not less than two or more than five years is the only penalty. It were well if these penalties were not almost obsolete. In the reports of the Commissioner of the State prison in Rhode Island, we find in the course of twenty-eight years, one solitary person imprisoned for that crime.* And our impression is both that there is no peculiar slackness

* A gentleman writes from a State where the penalty for adultery is a fine not exceeding one thousand dollars, or imprisonment not exceeding twelve months, as follows. "This offense is sometimes, but not often, punished by a *nominal* fine, and in case of negroes, I have known imprisonment added."

in executing the laws in that State, and that everywhere public opinion does not demand the infliction even of the pecuniary penalty. We are aware of the difficulties attending conviction for this crime, and the comparative innocence in some cases of the nominally offending party; but surely in the vast multitude of cases of divorce for adultery, many of which are blazoned before the eyes of men with disgusting publicity, there must be more deserving of punishment and capable of being convicted than are ever brought to justice. Meanwhile, private vengeance, unpunished and excused, is taking the place of public law: it would not be strange if more persons had been put to death within ten years past by injured husbands than the law has caught with its very gentle hooks. So it must ever be. Rude justice, violent, lawless, excessive retribution fills a vacuum from which the justice of society has leaked out. Let society forbear to punish homicide, and blood-revenge becomes an institution. Let it forbear to punish adultery, and the aggrieved kill the offenders, not merely when caught in the act, which law often authorizes, but on calculation and in cool blood.

We are not aware that any other species of injury done by one of the married parties to the other is made penal, except so far as the same kinds of wrong, on whomsoever inflicted, are punished by society.

There are disadvantages in respect to property, to which, especially when adultery is the ground of divorce, the guilty party or parties, against whom the divorce is issued, are exposed. Thus, according to the law of Maine, when the wife is an adulteress, the husband may hold both her personal estate forever, and the real estate also of which she was seized during coverture, it they had a living child born during marriage, and if not, during her life, in case he survives her. But the court may grant her so much of her real or personal estate as is necessary for her maintenance. Similar laws exist in Massachusetts, Rhode Island, and Michigan.* The law of Tennessee prescribes that the husband's rights, if he is the complainant, to his wife's property shall be the same as if marriage had continued. Others still leave the whole subject of alimony to the judge's discretion, or fix a limit beyond which it shall not reach, which limit, where the husband is guilty, must not in Rhode Island exceed half his real estate and half his personal. In Maine, if the husband is guilty, the wife is to have dower in his real estate, as if he were dead, and to have her own restored to her.

In regard to the power of the guilty party to contract a new marriage, the States differ exceedingly. Some lay no restrictions whatever on the liberty of divorced persons, so that, whether

* This law of Rhode Island refers to various kinds of offenses, those of other States, we believe, to adultery only.

complainants, or defendants, they are entirely free to marry one another again the next day, and the adulteress is free to marry anybody, even the partaker of her sin. Some of those States which in their laws authorize separations from bed and board, leave it to the parties—when the separation is perpetual —to become reconciled and to come together, while others put such reconciliation into the hands of the court, as a formal and solemn act. The following are some of the restrictions on the liberty of remarriage after divorce which we have noticed in the laws of the older States. It is in some of the States left to the courts to decide whether the offending party shall marry again. In Virginia a decree may forbid remarriage, but may afterward be revoked for sufficient cause. In Kentucky no such decree of remarriage can be legally made within five years. In Mississippi the law is as in Virginia, and in Missouri it is in any case of divorce as in Kentucky, with the additional proviso that the court may shorten this time of probation, but that such order must be made in a term subsequent to that in which the divorce was granted. In several States cohabitation after divorce brings on the parties divorced the penalty due to adultery. This is the case in Massachusetts, New Jersey, and Michigan. In others the offending party, or, it may be, the offending party where adultery furnishes ground for the divorce, cannot marry during the life-time of the other party.

Such a regulation we find in the laws of New York, North Carolina, Georgia, and Massachusetts; in which latter State such marriage, when unauthorized, ranks with polygamy in its penalty, but the judges may give liberty of remarriage if they see fit, on the petition of the guilty party, when the crime is not adultery. Finally, Louisiana, following the French code, prescribes that the offending party shall never marry the partner of his or her guilt, on pain of bigamy and of having such marriage pronounced a nullity. On the other hand, we have noticed no restrictions on the marriage of divorced persons in the laws of Maine, New Hampshire, Vermont, Rhode Island, Connecticut, Pennsylvania, Indiana, Illinois, and Alabama, while several of these States—Maine, Connecticut, Indiana—expressly declare the parties free to marry again.*

In looking back on the ground over which we have thus far traveled in this Chapter we perceive that the number of causes for which divorce may be obtained has been very considerably increased in modern times. There is an increasing

* It is quite possible that errors may have crept into the sketches of divorce legislation which we have presented to our readers. We have spent a good deal of time in consulting the complete collection of statutes in the State House at Hartford, where the State Librarian offers every facilty and assistance, but the hurry of taking notes, without the facility of verifying them afterward in cases of doubt, must bring with it more than one mistake. We shall be happy if some charitable reader will set us right.

desire to be free from the marriage bond on grounds which were, of old, regarded as insufficient; and an increasing willingness on the part of law-makers to gratify such a desire, as well as an increasing tendency to legislate on marriage as being a mere contract, to the neglect of its moral aspect. On the other hand, there is an impression in the mind of many persons that divorces, at least in a number of the States, are multiplying; that in a certain stratum of society—shall we call it Protestant society?—the feeling of the sanctity of marriage is passing away; that the highest crimes against that covenant which stands as a symbol of the union of Christ with his church, are either excused, or regarded as things of course, or even laughed at. Moral indignation, it is thought, no longer visits the adulterer or adulteress; the more vulgar newspapers joke about the crime, and divorced persons are no longer under that frown which met them formerly, even when divorced for causes below the greatest.

Is it true that divorces are increasing? Is it true that the number of them is at all equal to the number in those states in Europe where they are most freely granted? Is there any difference between the different States in the number of successful petitions for this privilege?

We propose to occupy the remainder of this Chapter with an exposition of the statistics of divorce as far as the tables prepared in several of the States place them within our reach. We regret to say that the materials are scanty. It is only of late that tables of births, deaths, and marriages have been begun in a portion of the States, while but a few are going a little farther into social or moral statistics. Massachusetts has published one list of divorces for five years, which is clumsily prepared, and leaves to the reader of it the work of counting and registering. In Vermont and in Connecticut the lists are more convenient, but in the latter State the causes of divorce have not been published with regularity. In Ohio the eminent commissioner of statistics, who has recently been displaced, Mr. Edward D. Mansfield, has prepared very useful tables. But in most of the other States all this information lies buried in the desks of the county clerks, and no one, probably, has taken the trouble to collect and make it known to the world. Some tables may have been drawn up with which we are unacquainted. Yet even our inadequate materials will supply some valuable results.

In these comparisons we may as well confess that we originally had the state of things in Connecticut in view, and were desirous of ascertaining how far this commonwealth differed, in one important department of morals, and in respect to one indication of social advance or decline, from its sister States. We were desirous, also, of finding out, if we could, whether there was any movement of divorce toward increase or diminution in number, and whether the law had any thing to do with such movement. This has been done once, and well done, by a friend of ours, in an article in the New Englander, entitled "Divorce Legislation in Connecticut," published in July, 1866.*

At the risk of repeating what was there said we must remind our readers that to the two original causes of divorce—adultery and desertion—there were added two others in 1843, "habitual intemperance and intolerable cruelty," and that in 1849 a new batch of causes was superadded, viz.: sentence of imprisonment for life, bestiality or any other infamous crime involving a violation of conjugal duty and punishable by imprisonment in the state-prison, and—what we have already spoken of—any such misconduct of the other party as permanently destroys the happiness of the petitioner and defeats the purposes of the marriage relation. This last is generally known in the State as the "omnibus clause." It appears that after each of these advances in legislation there was an increase of divorces, that the divorces in 1864 were five times as many as in 1849, although the population had grown by the addition of less than one-half, of which one-half Catholics, who did not swell the divorces, formed not a small part; and that the "omnibus" clause,

* See note 5 on Chapter V., at the end of this volume.

both directly and by its influence when other causes were weak, aided the petitioners for divorces not a little. Add to all this that after divorces are granted there is an unlimited license of remarriage, and that there is little fear of prosecutions for adultery. A man and woman once divorced may return to their old connection the next day.* The adulterer and his mistress, the adulteress and her paramour may be linked together in a union which they aimed, perhaps, to make possible by their crime. Herod and Herodias might live very comfortably under our laws, unless the tetrarch Philip were malicious enough not to sue for a divorce. Is it not time, if such is the case, to see whether we ought to warn our neighbors, or whether we had better advise them to follow our example. How, then do statistics show that we stand?

The statistics we shall present under the heads of the ratio of annual divorces to annual marriages, and, as far as we are able, to families and to population, and shall then seek to gather any lessons from them that they may convey.

In Vermont the ratio of annual divorces to annual marriages stands thus:

* A member of the committee raised to consider the subject of divorces in 1867 stated that he knew a couple in a town near his own who were divorced and married again a fortnight afterward, and obtained a second divorce on similar grounds with the first in a very short time.

Years.	Divorces.	Marriages.	Ratio.
1860,	94	2,179	1 to 23.2
1861,	65	2,188	" 33.7
1862,	94	1,962	" 21
1863,	102	2,007	" 20
1864,	98	1,804	" 18
1865,	122	2,569	" 21
1866,	155	3,001	" 19
Total,	730	15,710	" 21.5

In Massachusetts,

Years.	Divorces.	Marriages.	Ratios.
1861,	243	10,972	1 to 45
1862,	227	11,014	" 48.4
1863,	239	10,873	" 45.5
1864,	313	12,513	" 40
Total,	1,022	45,372	" 44.4

In Ohio (the years begin in July of the year named).

Years.	Divorces.	Marriages.	Ratios.
1865,	837	22,198	1 to 26
1866,	1,169	30,479	" 26
1867,	975		

In Connecticut,

Years.	Divorces.	Marriages.	Ratios.
1860,	310	3,978	1 to 12.83
1861,	275	3,757	" 13.70
1862,	257	3,701	" 14.44
1863,	291	3,467	" 11.90
1864,	426	4,107	" 9.64
1865,	404	4,460	" 11.04
1866,	488	4,978	" 10.19
1867,	459	4,779	" 10.40
Total,	2,910	33,227	" 11.40*

From Prussia we have some materials for instituting a comparison between that country of notoriously loose divorce laws and the States named above. We exclude the Catholic population, which cannot be done with accuracy in the States,

* We give here from Rev. H. Loomis's article the divorces from 1849 to 1859, with some other matter touching the state of divorce in Connecticut. These tables are taken, as we understand, from the records in the several counties.

Years.	*Divorces.*	*Years.*	*Divorces.*
1849	91	1855	208
1850	129	1856	215
1851	165	1857	232
1852	159	1858	256
1853	186	1859	299
1854	216		

In 498 divorces, 169 were granted on petition of the husband, 329 on that of the wife.

Of these 192 were granted before six years of marriage had expired, 306 afterward.

and thus the story which the tables tell is unfairly in favor of the latter. For instance, in Connecticut, where the whole number of marriages was, as before stated, 4,978 in 1866, the marriages, in which both parties were of foreign birth, were 1,208. Now of these it is safe to say that two-thirds, say 800, were Catholics, who rarely petition for divorce in this State. Deducting them we have the ratio of one divorce to less than eight and a half of so called Protestant or rather non-Catholic marriages.

Prussia, in 1855. Marriages of non-Catholics, 84,914; divorces, 2,937: ratio, 1 to 29.

Thus Connecticut is at the bottom of the list altogether. The ratio of divorces to marriages is here double what it is in Vermont, nearly four-fold that in Massachusetts, and much more than double that in Prussia. There are absolutely more divorces in Connecticut, on the average, by 108 (viz.; 364 every year) than in Massachusetts, a State with two and a half times as many inhabitants. There were in 1866, more than half as many as in Ohio, a State with almost five times the population.

It ought to be said that the divorces in several of the States were unduly great in the year 1864, and have been so since the war. The reason must be that many hasty marriages were contracted by soldiers; the motive being on the woman's part, to get a share of the bounty, or the pension, if the husband should be killed. But to counterbalance this, the marriages, as always happens in similar cases after a war, have increased quite perceptibly, so that the ratio is not much affected.

In Prussia the comparisons are made between the number of divorces and the whole number of married couples, or between the divorces and the whole population. The statistics which have fallen under our notice are the following, pertaining to 1838–1840.

Judicial	district of	Berlin,	57	divorces	to 100,000	inhabitants.
"	"	Frankfort,	30	"	"	"
"	"	Magdeburg,	35	"	"	"
"	"	Konigsberg,	34	"	"	"
"	"	Stettin,	36,	"	"	"
"	"	Greifswald,	16	"	"	"

In the Rhine provinces, among 600,000 Protestants, there were four divorces to 100,000 souls, which last item shows that in a Prussian province, where the general Code is not used, but the legislation is based on the Code Napoleon, and the people have had a different juristic training, the divorces are very few. Or in other words the Prussian divorce law encourages and multiplies divorces. This is shown also by the tables for other parts of Protestant Germany. Thus, in Saxony, in judicial districts, containing 900,000 inhabitants, taking the average of 1836–1840, there were not quite 19 divorces to 100,000 souls. In Electoral Hesse there were in 1835, 24; in 1841, 23; in 1851, 16; in 1852, 17; in 1853, 14 divorces, which point to ratios varying between less than 4 and 2 to 100,000.*

Our comparisons of these data with similar ones in some of the United States must be based in part on estimates. For Massachusetts, we follow Dr. Jarvis's estimates in the census of that State for 1865 (page 206). Vermont adds to its population so slowly that the United States census of 1860 may be taken to represent the present number of inhabitants. For Connecticut, we may calculate on a yearly addition of two per cent., which is about the same increase which prevailed between 1850 and 1860, but which may be too small, so that the ratio would need to be slightly reduced.†

* From Strippelmann's Ehescheidungsrecht, a valuable work written by a lawyer at Cassel in Hesse, and published in 1854. Our authority for the other German statistics is Viebahn's Statistik, part 2, published in 1862. The American authorities are the annual reports of the Commissioners of Statistics in Ohio for 1855–57, a report submitted to the Legislature of Massachusetts in 1856, embracing five years, from 1860 to 1864, the State Librarian's annual reports in Connecticut, which for several years have by law embraced divorces also, and for Vermont the public reports for 1860, 1861, and a manuscript detailed statement kindly furnished by Henry Clark, Esq., of Rutland, Clerk of the Senate of that State. Rev. W. W. Andrews and others have rendered us important assistance.

† This would give to the State nearly 528,000 inhabitants in 1867. A calculation from the number of children in the school districts for whom money could be drawn—of whom there were in 1860 105,460 to 460,147 inhabitants, and in 1867, 120,884—would give about 537,000. But the ratio of children to the whole popula-

In Vermont, taking the average, as already given, there is one divorce annually to 3,125 inhabitants, 33 divorces to 100,000.

In Massachusetts, there were, in

1861, 19.7 divorces to 100,000.
1862, 18.2 " "
1863, 19. " "
1864, 24.8 " "

In Ohio, in 1865, there were 33⅓ divorces to 100,000.

And in Connecticut, in

1860, 67.4 divorces to 100,000.
1864, 85.5 " "
1867, 87.5 " "

But this, bad as it is, as we said, tells too good a story, for our estimate of population embraces all the Catholics.

In Prussia, again, as the following table shows, the divorces are steadily decreasing, owing, as Viebahn says, to the more "earnest treatment" of divorces on the part of the civil and church authorities. The table gives the number of divorces and of married couples at several intervals.

1818, 3,138 divorces, 1 to 517 existing marriages.
1822, 2,832 " " 617 "
1836, 3,291 " " 593 "
1839, 2,789 " " 731 "

tion is decreasing, hence the population may be regarded as higher still in 1867. This would give about 85.5 to 100,000, instead of 87.5 for 1867, as stated in the text.

1841,	2,714	divorces,	1 to	774	existing	marriages.
1850,	2,920	"	"	798	"	"
1855,	2,937	"	"	965	"	"

This, however, indicates not the married couples among the Protestants, as it ought to do, but through the entire population. To get at the former, we should have to diminish the last list in about the ratio of 16 to 10. Thus, in 1855, it would be, instead of 1 to 965, 1 to 603.

We have no statistics of the number of married couples in this country, but the number of families is given in the last census of Massachusetts, and the average there found, of 4.7 to a family, will probably apply to the New England States in general. Then we should have to deduct those families at the head of which there is not a married pair, in order to make a comparison with Prussia; but to perform this process we have no data within our reach. The number of families, however, in Massachusetts, in 1865, was 269,968, and the ratio here would be for 1864 one divorce to 862 families. In Connecticut for the same year, there was one to less than 249 families.

Thus, Connecticut, according to all of these measures of its position, occupies a bad eminence among the States.* We should be glad to have

* Indiana and Missouri certainly have no statistics of divorce, and we suppose the same to be true of all the Western States. A friend residing in Indiana estimates the annual divorces there to be almost 2,000. If it be so, the ratio to the number of in-

it in our power to present more exact statistics touching the ratio of divorce to families, for it is the disease that undermines family life. The eminent commissioner of statistics for Ohio, in his report for 1865, has some striking remarks on this great social evil. The number of divorces for that year was 837, which, says he, "at the present population of the State, is 1 to 3,000 persons, and 1 divorce to 26 of the annual number of marriages. It is not a very pleasant thought, that, when we look upon twenty-six couples of young married people, we know that one of those couples must be divorced. Yet such is the state of fact. To begin with a marriage, we have these facts. One of every 60 persons we shall meet on a road will be married within a year. But as one-half of the population are under the marriageable age, and more than half the residue are married, it follows that at least one in fifteen of all the marriageable people we meet will be married within a year, or two persons out of each thirty of a marriageable age, will be married in a year —giving one marriage to each thirty. Twenty-six times that is 780; and thus two persons out of 780, or one out of 390 of all the marriageable

habitants surpasses that of Connecticut. It has been lately asserted in print that somewhat over 400 divorces were granted in the city of Chicago within one year, 1868 we believe. This is a great number; but the large towns far exceed the average in this respect.

people in the State, will be married and divorced in a year. This is the ratio, although the actual divorce will probably not take place for several years."

A somewhat similar train of thought has occurred to us in regard to Connecticut, where, for several years, one divorce has taken place to about ten marriages. Deduct now the Catholics, deduct also the better class of society, than whom a class more observant of the family tie exists nowhere on earth, and we shall conclude that out of every seven couples that call themselves Protestants one will be divorced, while according to Mr. Loomis's tables in the New Englander, July, 1866, two-thirds of the divorces will occur in less than six years after marriage. And we believe that the present law must bear the burden of this social immorality.

But we cannot help adding one comparison more. Dr. Dwight, in his sermon on divorce,* says that when the flood-gates were opened at the outbreak of the French revolution, there were, according to the Abbé Gregoire, 20,000 divorces granted in France in about a year and a half. Now, there were, it is said, in 1791, about twenty-six millions of persons in France. Suppose now that two-thirds of these divorces belonged to one year. According to the rate in Connecticut in 1866, there ought to have been in France over

* Theology, Sermon 121.

26,000, or according to the rate in France there ought to have been less than 266 instead of 488 that year in Connecticut. If things go on so, people will begin to wish that the lower classes, among whom now divorces principally prevail, could come under Catholic influence.

We have little to add to this exposition. The causes of divorce are given in the various reports presented to the legislatures. Some of the information we annex. In Vermont, out of 571 divorces in five years, there were for adultery, 164; willful desertion, 188; desertion, 60; intolerable severity, 126; for refusal to support, 13; with 20 others, in most of which more causes than one are mentioned. In Massachusetts, out of 1,294 divorces granted in about five years, there were for adultery, 546, or 42.3 per cent.; for desertion, 589, or 45.6 per cent.; for cruelty, 122, or 9.4 per cent.; 15 for intemperance, and 21 miscellaneous. Here the large ratio for adultery is startling. Can this represent the real state of the case? In Ohio, out of 2,601 cases of which the causes are particularly assigned, there were granted for adultery, 935; for absence and neglect, 1,030; for cruelty, 440; for intemperance, 196. For Connecticut, we add to Mr. Loomis's tables those published by the State Librarian for 1866–7, borrowing his remark in his report for 1866, that the causes far exceed the number of divorces granted. These causes are mainly

	1866.	1867.
Adultery,	158	118
Desertion,	193	153
Cruelty,	91	78
Misconduct,	177	190
Intemperance,	91	91
	710	630

"The foregoing table of causes is wholly unreliable," says the Librarian in his report of 1867, and only so much seems to be deducible, that the cause of "misconduct" under the *omnibus* clause of the act of 1849, is exerting increasing mischief, helping out other grounds where they are weak, and having a baleful because a most indefinite and capricious influence of its own.

In Vermont, again, the husband is the libellant in 266 and the wife in 315 cases; in Massachusetts, if we have counted right, the husband in 428 cases and the wife in 866; and in Connecticut in the years 1866–67, the husband in just one-third, the wife in two-thirds of the cases reported, which were 810 in number.

Of the number of cases presented to the courts and rejected—which if published might test the strictness of the courts—we have no accounts, except that in Ohio, in 1867, 1,441 petitions came before the courts, of which 975 were granted, 245 dismissed, and 220 not disposed of at the close of the statistical year.

Of the origin of the applicants for divorce we have no items furnished to us, save that in Ohio the counties where the Catholics form a considerable part of the population fell below their ratio, while the "Western Reserve counties have a much larger proportion of divorces than the rest of the State." These counties constitute "New Connecticut," the settlers of which came from the old State. The fact is significant.

Has it not, we ask in closing, been made to appear that the laws of divorce in this country demand a thorough examination, and, in many States at least, a thorough revision, but especially in that State formerly the land of steady habits, where the law and the habits of the people show the greatest degeneracy.* And are not all the churches, all right-minded people, all Protestants and Catholics, called upon to unite in a de-

*In 1867 a committee of the legislature of Connecticut reported an act touching divorce, which was not passed but referred over to the next legislature as unfinished business. It contains some remedies for the defects of the present law, but they touch only minor evils. Section 1 requires, where the application for divorce is *ex parte*, the testimony of two credible witnesses residing in the State, to the good character and residence in the State of the applicant. Section 2 requires that no divorce cases shall be heard in chambers or elsewhere than in open court and in the regular court-room. Section 3 forbids granting divorce on the ground of misconduct, until one year after the commencement of the suit, and Section 4 forbids granting it for any other reason until six months after passing the decree, which is to be void unless the time for its taking effect be expressed therein.

mand that there be some check on so great and threatening an evil as that which we have spoken of in this chapter. What the duty of Christian churches is in regard to divorce, especially in their discipline, and what are the leading features of a good, or at least an endurable divorce law, we intend to consider in our next and closing chapter.

CHAPTER VI.

ATTITUDE OF THE CHURCH TOWARD DIVORCE LAWS: PRINCIPLES OF DIVORCE LEGISLATION.

In closing our essay on the subject of divorce, we come to a very important field of inquiry; to the relation, namely, between the view of divorce taken by the law of the land and that which is taken by Christian morals, and to the questions, what are the obligations of the Christian Church as to this matter, and what are the true principles of a healthy divorce-legislation. We shall touch on these points in the order named with all possible brevity, and not without the hope of helping in some slight degree as well the cause of sound morality as that of sound legislation.

Marriage, as the starting point of the family and of the state, as a divine institution established both in our nature and by positive precept, and as involving the welfare of mutually dependent beings, has and must have important relations to religion, morality, and law. Religion strives to throw a sanctity around it both by the ceremonies with which it is solemnized, and by the guilt which is made to attach to adultery. In other words, religion stands up in defense of the morality of the family state, and this it does in many heathen societies, as well as under the light of Christianity. So also law starts from a feeling of the sanctity of marriage; it is built on a moral conviction at its very beginning. There are sacred obligations which are violated by adultery and must be protected. The question whether a man can have more than one wife is determined by the state of moral feeling in the community. Divorce cannot in fact be separated from the ends and uses of marriage which lie within the province of morals, and adultery cannot and never has been regarded as a mere breach of contract. And so the better the laws are, the more they watch over and exact the fulfillment of those obligations to which marriage gives rise by bringing new beings into the world.

Marriage is sometimes regarded as a contract, and it is very common to draw false inferences from the assumption that it is such. If it be only a contract, it is natural to argue that it may cease at the will of the parties, as for instance after a certain number of years, or on failure of having children, or when inclination for each other has ceased; just as other contracts—those of service, partnership, or loan for instance—take the special form imposed on them by the contracting parties. And so, as contract is one of the commonest of the modes of intercourse, it has been used to explain and to belittle both the church and the state. It has entered into theology, and has put a covenant made by God with Adam into the place of a great law of race and a divine economy. The state has been built on compact, made as if by men who had lived alone before. In the case of marriage the particular parties do indeed make a contract, but it contemplates an entrance into a special definite mode ot moral and social life, which the contract cannot essentially modify; just as the voluntary nature of the church presupposes such an unalterable type of church existence as Christ and the Apostles laid down, and as the state, in all its free varying forms, presupposes the recognition of justice and the protection of the individual.

Marriage then is more than a contract, and must be regarded by right law to have this nature. So the Romans regarded it. The well-known definition of Modestinus, the eminent scholar of Ulpian at the beginning of the third century, as well as the similar one of the Institutes which has passed into canonical law, contemplates the perpetuity of the marriage union of one man and one woman as essential to the nature of the institution. It runs as follows: Nuptiæ sunt conjunctio maris et fœminæ et consortium omnis vitæ, divini et humani juris communicatio.*

* Comp. Inst. Justin, 1–9, § 2. "Nuptiæ sive matrimonium

And from the general principle contained in this definition no legislation of Christian lands for a long time together has diverged. It condemns polygamy, it frowns on divorce. The union of a marriage pair must at least continue until a formal act of the State shall pronounce it ended by some misconduct of one of the pair toward the other.

But although Christian morality and a state where faith in Christ prevails will take fundamentally the same view of marriage, yet the state may require in certain minor points that which the church forbids, or forbid that which the church either ordains or allows, or it may at least allow that which the church disapproves. The first procedure may be illustrated by the conflict between civil marriage and the sacramental theory of the Roman Church. The law of France, and of other lands which have adopted French views, requires all persons contracting marriage to go through a form of civil contract before a magistrate, and then the marriage is *legitimum*. As for the rest, it leaves to their own consciences whether they shall apply to the priest, the minister of the sacrament, for the solemnization of their union, so that it may be *ratum* according to the

est viri et mulieris conjunctio, individuam vitæ consuetudinem continens." In the decree of Gratian, part 2, Caus. xxvii., Quaest. ii., c. 3, we have the definition "consensus ergo cohabitandi et individuam vitæ consuetudinem retinendi interveniens eos conjuges fecit. Individua vero vitæ consuetudo est talem se in omnibus exhibere viro, qualis ipsa sibi est, et e converso."

church view. The Catholic Church has been obliged to endure this, although it considers the separation of the civil contract and the sacrament to be inadmissible, since the contracting parties are the administrators of the sacrament. And with this feeling the Concordat between the Pope and Austria, made a few years since, did away, we believe, with the civil contract, which within this present year the force of public opinion has restored to its former place in the laws.* So also a state may prevent marriages which are valid according to church law from having validity by civil law, as must happen if it admit into its legislation a greater number of cases of nullity than the ecclesiastical law recognizes.

But these cases of conflict between state and church law are of minor importance, especially in Protestant countries; the most common atti tude of the state, outside of the thoroughly Catholic lands, is to sanction by its legislation that which the doctrine of the New Testament and the general sentiment of Christian churches condemns. Here there is properly no conflict. The state says to the church in regard to marriage and divorce, you must take your own course and provide for the purity of life and discipline by your own measures. The state is not bound to extend its legislation over all the departments of morality, still less is it required to protect religion by puni-

* Comp. Richter Kirchenr., 6th ed., § 263.

tive statutes. We do not, in societies which have advanced far beyond the simplicity of the family state, generally punish lying or drunkenness, or filthy words or sabbath-breaking, or other outward offenses which a church may fairly notice by its discipline. Why is it obligatory on the state in the case of marriage and divorce to follow the strict rule laid down in the New Testament? Were the state to require what Christian doctrine forbids, or forbid what the church requires, it would be tyrannical, it would be at war with a power co-ordinate with itself, in the end it would perish; but when it simply allows married persons to separate from one another for causes not recognized by Christ, it lays no burden on tender consciences, it comes into no conflict with religion, it leaves the remedy against the evils of an imperfect moral code in the hands of the church, which is the main support of morality in Christian lands.

We admit the justice of the position that the state is not bound to forbid many things which the individual may do in his outward actions which are sins in the sight of God, and even injurious, on the whole, to society. There is a difference between doing this and legalizing what is considered by Christian people to be contrary to the law of the New Testament. All that they ask is, that, in the matter of divorce the state should abstain from action; that it should enact no laws making immoral separations legal, and thus giving a bounty to immorality. When the state imposes no penalty on drunkenness, or lying, or sabbath-breaking, its attitude is simply negative. And here it does not cut off a remedy, if, by either of these sins a man inflicts an injury on others, as through violent assault, or slander, or disturbance of the public peace. But when it grants a divorce for a year's desertion, for instance, or for misconduct destroying the happiness of the marriage relation, its action is positive. It removes from the obligations of the marriage relation persons who otherwise would be under them; it grants the power of marrying again to persons who otherwise would have no such power. Its action, therefore, is not at all like its inaction in cases of individual immorality.

And there is, moreover, a difference between the effects of the two. When sabbath-breaking is not punished by civil law no one would infer that the state thought it right, but, when divorce is allowed for causes confessedly not sanctioned by the New Testament, the state steps forward as a teacher of an opposite morality from that of the New Testament. Owing to the manifold relations of marriage, as well to the civil condition as to morality and to religion, people will be very apt to feel that divorce is perfectly right, and the influence of bad doctrine thus taught by the state will run over within the pale of the church, to divorce it from Christ's law, to trouble it with many perplexing questions, to injure its discipline and its purity. This must be true in Catholic lands, if the law of the church and the law of the state are at variance; how much more must it be so in Protestant or mixed countries, where there is no such distinct and sweeping law of church action as the Catholic doctrine of the sacramental quality of marriage.

The law of the state, as it seems to us, can take only one of two positions in regard to marriage: either it must teach that it is neither bound nor inclined to support Christian law, or that there is such an inveterate leaning toward divorce, that the evils from a stricter law would be greater than those which attend the present loose one. That this is a good ground for imperfect legislation, we admit; but what a confession of impotence and of a corrupt civilization to be obliged to go back to the customs of a half-barbarous society like that of the Jews under Moses, and to own that the ennobling conceptions of Christ, which must influence law if they are generally entertained, have even as yet no practical sway. Moreover, what if it should turn out that the laws themselves, by their own bad qualities, have multiplied divorces and corrupted opinion. New York and Connecticut, contiguous States, differ vastly in their divorce legislation. Is there naturally any greater "hardness of hearts" on this side of Byram River to account for this difference, or is it due to the unwariness and unskillfulness of legislators?

But whatever be the attitude of the State, the Church must stand upon the principles of the New Testament as she expounds them, and apply them to all who are within her reach. The minister, if his celebration of marriage be not a farce, can no more join in marriage two persons who, in his view, have no right to form such a union, than he can aid any other immoral proceeding. Suppose the persons intending such a union to be a woman put away for other cause than that of adultery, and a man, whoever he be, to whom our Saviour's words would have application—"that he who marrieth her who is put away committeth adultery." How can the fact, that such a union is legal, in the least degree justify a minister of Christ in giving a religious sanction to an act which he believes to be an adulterous one? Ought he not to say, in solemnizing such a union, "whom God hath *not joined* together let not man put asunder." Or can the minister take the ground that he is merely an official person in solemnizing marriage, whose duty extend only to the point of throwing the influence of religion around the commencement of a most important relation; while the question whether the two persons who ask for his blessing upon their nuptials have the responsibility of deciding whether their union is legal and Christian. But if he carried out this principle he would be an official person, and nothing more, in celebrating the Lord's Supper, and thus any one who wished ought to have free admission to the Lord's table. There could then be no discipline, because, even in the case of gross offenders, it must needs be left to themselves whether they have repented or not. In the case of celebrating marriage, the minister's duty is comparatively easy. A specific act is requested of him by persons whose past life is generally notorious, whose former relations are matter of common fame, if there be any thing scandalous about them. The question of what they think right is of minor importance for him. He might as well indorse a forged note on the ground that it must be left to the conscience of the forger to decide upon the morality of his act, as to help two persons to enter into a union which he regards as adulterous, on the same ground. In the case of giving access to all to the Lord's table, the principle in question would be more justifiable, because in the strictest churches much must be left to individual consciences just at that point. But it is a false principle in all ministerial acts, and would, if allowed, destroy the purity, if not the life, of the Christian Church.

The duty of the minister, in the case supposed, seems to be clear. There is another and a more important point to be considered in reference to the duty of the Christian Church in the treatment of those of its members, who, under the law of the state, contract or dissolve marriages against the law of Christ. This we say, is the most important question, and it is so for two reasons. The first is, that in all countries where a civil marriage is required, or where—as in many parts of this country—a marriage performed by some civil authority, has the same validity as one celebrated by a minister of the gospel, the refusal of the minister to act in a certain case has no great bearing, since the civil authorities can take his place. The minister satisfies his own conscience; perhaps he awakens discussion in his parish, and that is all. But a loose, unchristian habit of the Christian Church, or of Christian churches in a community, in reference to marriage and divorce, sets up an insurmountable obstacle to the recognition and observance of Christ's law of marriage. It excuses bad civil legislation; it inculcates bad principles on the members of the church; it fails to teach what it ought to teach, what principles of discipline were designed to teach. Practically it supports the state in its attitude of disregard to Christian law. It thus tends to break up the spirit of discipline, to put to silence the voice of the church in favor of holiness, and to take away its power of standing up in the world as the main support of Christian morals.

The other reason for the importance of this inquiry in regard to the duty of the church, as it respects divorce, is to be found in the occasional difficulty of the questions which may present themselves. Or, in other words, until state law comes nearer to Christ's law, and until the churches cease to regard the state law of divorce as their standard of morality, multitudes of persons will be entrapped into forming unions which Christ forbids. These cases, and especially certain hard cases, where the unchristian marriage was long since consummated, may cause extreme perplexity to such as desire to obey Christ, and at the same time are aware how harsh and grinding invariable rules of discipline must be, especially in a period of transition from a loose neglect to healthy observance of Christian rules.

We say "a period of transition," implying thus that at present in this country Christian discipline in the matter of divorce by no means attempts to execute the law of the gospel. Is not this so? Has not the looseness in the matter of divorce passed over from the state to the church? As the one holds that its only concern in questions of divorce is the maintenance of individual rights, with a certain supervision of the welfare of society, does not the other, to a great extent, refer such questions to the consciences of the parties who have, by divorce or by marrying divorced persons, sinned against Christ's law? So far as we can learn, all Protestant churches in this country are loose and negligent in such cases. There are none, indeed, that would not exclude adulterers from the communion, even though the State rarely attempts to inflict its slight penalties for this crime. But there are few cases, we apprehend, where persons legally married receive church censures, however unchristian their relation may be, whether judged by Christ's law, or by Paul's rule, as generally interpreted. This slackness of discipline may have arisen from the extreme rarity of such cases among the members of the church: for a long time there was no especial reason for deciding what was the meaning of the commands given by Christ or by his apostles, since cases of divorce within the church, if known at all, were for adultery and desertion alone. Even after the state abandoned the Christian position usually taken by Protestants, the practice of divorce was confined to the more unprincipled classes of society. The church was thus taken unawares, and its lay members, naturally thinking that divorce is a matter of state legislation, overlooking the religious side of marriage and the precepts of the New Testament, and regarding it in the light of a civil contract, were prepared for any slackness of discipline which was not intolerable. The ministers, we judge, are more enlightened than the laity, and a reform in discipline may be more difficult in those forms of Protestantism where "the power of the keys" is intrusted to the congregation than in those where the eldership and the minister, or the latter alone, exercise this authority, according to a general law of the particular denomination. Within a brief period, several cases have come to our knowledge where ministers in Congregational churches refused to sanction marriages of divorced persons, and several others where the church sustained the looser view of divorce contained in State law against the opinion of the minister, who, in one instance, resigned his place on account of the collision. In another case, an association of ministers refused to recommend one of their number to another body, because, in their opinion, he had put away his wife unlawfully. As the Congregational churches have always been comparatively strict in sustaining the discipline of the New Testament, it is likely that they will be, many of them, the foremost to restore it in case of divorce, while others of them will be the last to abandon a habit of slackness which the New Testament condemns.

Our impression then is, that Christian churches in this country do not stand where they ought; that the cause of this, in part at least, is the insensible influence of bad State law; that the ministers, as a body, are aware of the evil affecting and threatening the purity and gospel order of their churches, but that many of the laity within the church overlook the law of Christ entirely. It is cheering and a source of hope for the future welfare of society, to observe that great bodies of Christians are moving for reform and for return to the old usage in respect to the discipline of divorce. We have had occasion to know that for some time many of the ministers of the Congregational churches in Connecticut have had their thoughts turned in this direction. The Episcopal Convention of Connecticut held at Middletown, in June, 1868, considered the same subject and expressed their sense of the evil of existing State legislation in decided resolutions. The Methodist Church, North, also, at their late triennial meeting in Chicago, embraced divorce within the topics of discussion; and although no general law of that church, as far as we can learn, was passed, the attention given to this point is a favorable sign.

But no action has been, as yet, so decided and so promising for the future as that of the triennial convention of the Protestant Episcopal Church, which was held at New York in October and November of 1868. The result of the discussions in relation to divorce was the following canon:

> "No minister of this church shall solemnize matrimony in any case where there is a divorced wife or husband of either party still living; but this canon shall not be held to apply to the innocent party in a divorce for the cause of adultery, or to parties once divorced seeking to be united again."

It appears from the debates in the House of Deputies, that some members—perhaps not a few—were willing to go further, and prohibit all remarriage of divorced persons. The canon imposes no obligation on them to act against their convictions.

This canon, which is, we believe, the first legislation of the Episcopal Church in the matter in hand, repeats a resolution passed some sixty years since. We rejoice in its passage, while we make, in the way of friendly criticism, several remarks, of which the *first* is, that the canon allows the marriage of a guilty party divorced for adultery after the death of the innocent one, and that even to the partner in guilt. Perhaps it was wise to say nothing of this case which is noticed by ancient canonical laws. 2. It allows ministers to unite a divorced couple a second time. But if they are still husband and wife, why solemnize their union over again. Does not the canon admit the validity of their divorce when it authorizes ministers to unite them again, or is there an intentional ambiguity in the word *unite*, which can mean marriage or something less, and so can suit various shades of opinions? Furthermore, the canon would not only allow the reunion to one another of persons divorced on account of the adultery of one of the parties, but also that of a divorced wife to her first husband, even after the termination of a marriage to a second husband by divorce or by his death. The ancient church would not have disliked the reunion in the first instance, after condonation, yet would never have thought of remarriage; while the union supposed in the second case would have been monstrous even to a Jew, and would have "greatly polluted" the land. 3. In practice the minister must generally be guided by the decrees of the courts of law. But a decree in many of our courts on the score of adultery, is no proof that the crime was ever committed. 4. For the minister's conscience the canon is an excellent one; but what if the parties get themselves joined in marriage by a careless or unscrupulous minister of another denomination, and then appear in their pew or at the Lord's table. What will the Episcopal minister do in their case? If they are not disciplined, the canon becomes *brutum fulmen.* But ministers may forbear to discipline, and so another canon seems necessary to support the one already passed.

But as long as the church follows the law of Christ, and the state makes another law dissolving marriage on slighter grounds, there will be frequent cases of legal but unchristian divorce and marriage. What is the duty of the church when such cases arise in which one of the parties at least is a member of the church, and amenable to its discipline?

First, we may take the ground that the parties in unchristian divorce and marriage have acted according to their own views of duty, and ought to be undisturbed. This might be a sound rule of action if the rule in the Scriptures were not a clear one; if the churches had not formally re-affirmed the rule as their basis of discipline—as we suppose them to have done—and if there were no important social reasons for giving it all possible support. It is hardly conceivable that, when the apostle bids the Christian wife, who has for certain causes departed from her husband, to be reconciled to him or remain unmarried, he did not take it for granted that a violation of this command would be visited with church censures. It is still less conceivable that when Christ calls putting away a wife for any cause short of her fornication by the name of adultery, he did not intend that it should be treated as such, by his church at least, if not by the state. For these are tangible open acts, not like states of mind capable of two interpretations, but ascertainable by the ordinary rules of evidence. Moreover, the individuals concerned, after the church or churches shall have taken a position, can no longer plead ignorance or the excuse of legality. Add to this that there is no barrier against bad law, no adequate protection of society within the sphere of those relations with which both church and state have to do, unless the church not only gives its advice in the way of a general rule, but makes use also of the single weapon of self-defense and of terror to evil-doers that is within its reach—exclusion from its privileges. Let the law not forbid polygamy, and let a man with four or with many wives seek to enter the Christian Church. Is not the benefit to society of a protest against polygamy, and of a refusal to admit a polygamist into or to continue him in the church so great, that there could be no doubt how the church ought to act in a case like this? Ought a change of the law, which forbids more than one wife, to make Christians feel that discipline should be slackened in such cases, or ought not this change to be a reason rather for enforcing discipline?

We conceive, then, that no believer in the gospel and in the duty of retaining purity among believers, can dissent from our position, that in cases of marriage and divorce where the Christian law is violated, the church ought to interfere—to prevent by its authority, and to censure by that essential power of excluding unworthy members, which belongs to all societies, even of the most voluntary character. The Catholic Church is not to be blamed for the ground it has taken in this matter. Its law of divorce may have gone beyond that of the gospel. Its system of prohibited degrees is an addition to Christian morality, as is confessed by the frequency of dispensations; but assuredly it is not wrong in refusing to make the law of the state its basis of action concerning divorce rather than the law of Christ, nor in feeling itself called, whatever be the law of the state, to educate the people and protect its own principles by ecclesiastical censures.

But secondly, while recent cases of divorce or of marriage with a person unlawfully divorced may be of easy handling, when once the rules of the church are distinctly laid down, there still remains a class of cases which call for a separate consideration. We refer to cases where the offense against the Christian rule of marriage occurred long since, where the parties in their irreligiousness only aimed to keep within the law of the state, and have for years reputably sustained the relations of man and wife, but now, having at last felt the influence of the gospel, are seeking to become members of some church of Christ. If they had lived in concubinage, the case would present no difficulty, for solemn marriage would repair the fault, they might repent and do honor to the sacred laws of morality by turning their condition into one allowed by God and by Cæsar both. But in the case supposed, where the sin of the individuals concerned was one of thoughtlessness at first, where the existing relation is not only permitted but the severance of it is forbidden by civil laws, what position shall the church take? Shall it take the position of the Catholic Church and require the entire discontinuance of their union, at least until the death of a previous husband and wife, or the similar position of the extreme abolitionist, who, because slavery originates in wrong, would require all slave-holders, under all circumstances, to make their slaves free or be cast out of the church? Shall it, we say, take this rigorous view of practical morality, or shall it say that cases may arise, where, by a sort of equity, the ordinary rule ought to be set aside, or where there is a sort of prescription against the original and in favor of the existing condition. We confess ourselves to be of this latter opinion, and to hold that the positive precept of marriage, like some other positive precepts, must bend to the necessities of the case. The peculiarities in such extreme cases, where the marriage relation is concerned, are due in part to the fact that marriage has a civil as well as a religious side,—that the state may even forbid the separation of persons who ought never to have been united in marriage at the outset; and in part to the fact that marriage itself brings the parties to it into a unique relation, a relation exclusive, most intimate, and often involving the highest interests of children. We take in fact the same ground which the Catholic Church takes in regard to prohibited degrees of consanguinity or affinity. The general rule is valuable, but there may be reasons for dispensation. As for prohibited degrees, the dispensation comes before the marriage, but there can be no permission beforehand, no consent of the church to such marriages as we now have in view. Such consent can only come afterward, when the married pair forsake a life of ungodliness and seek the privileges of Christians. But the case differs from some which may present themselves when heathen seek admission into the society of Christ. A man must leave all his wives except the first, or, at least, except one, both because polygamy is directly opposed to the spirit of the gospel, and because it would almost ruin a newly founded church to allow part of its members to have many wives while others have but one. In the case, however, which we have supposed, the couple continue with a Christian spirit a union which began without it, they honor the holiness of the church by repentance, and a *restitutio ad integrum* is impossible.

But it may be said that there is a very plain course for parties, thus married against the strictness of Christian law, to take. Let them separate and lead a life of continence apart. This would be the Catholic way of cutting the knot. But here there are two obvious difficulties, the disaster to children from breaking up the family state, and the perils of an enforced celibacy. A better way, in our judgment, where such peculiar cases arise, is to consent to the state *de facto*. It may be right even for the usurper, in a certain condition of a people, to continue his sway against all justice, when his power has stood the test of years, and all the relations of society have conformed themselves to the altered state of things. The same holds good in the case which we have been considering. Let the church, while it cannot be a party to any violation of Christ's law, accept an old condition of things within certain limits without seeking to tear up or overthrow.

As long as the state legislates on one set of principles and the church on another, there must be a conflict between the two powers, or else the church must succumb, for the state has the outward positive relations of life under its control. But the two powers may be brought near to one another, so as at least not to come into frequent conflict by the efforts of the church to teach the true doctrine concerning marriage and divorce, and by its healthy discipline over its members. There will then remain those pariahs of society who lie outside of all Christian influences and care nothing for the sanctity of marriage, and those civilized, refined heathens, who look on marriage as a mere contract, or as a respectable kind of concubinage. Even now divorce and marriage with a person divorced against the rules of the New Testament are principally confined to these classes. It is for the benefit of these classes, then, and in order to fulfill its office of purifying instead of corrupting society that the law of divorce needs extensive reformations and improvements. The Protestant churches, if once awake to present evils, for which State law and a low conception of marriage are accountable, can take care of themselves and of the interests put into their hands. But how far ought a reformation to be carried and at what ought reformers to aim? A Christian would be glad to have an end put to all conflict and possibility of conflict between the two authorities, to have divorce or separation granted only on account of adultery and malicious desertion, or for the first reason alone. In the present state of Christian countries, however, this extent of reformation is altogether unlikely to be attained. In this country especially, where the divine in government and in social life is so generally overlooked, where doctrine concerning the state and the relations of men so generally takes the vulgar, apprehensible form of contract, where the desire of speedy enjoyment and the quick procurement of the means of it are degrading the moral sentiments, it cannot be expected that reforms of our divorce laws will be very thorough. Law-makers will say that they are not bound by the morality of the New Testament in their legislation touching rights and the common welfare, that you may as well separate two parties who hate and injure one another rather than vainly strive to reach the inaccessible ideal by your laws which the next legislature can alter, and that strictness in prohibiting divorce will not prevent social evil but will only force it to pour its fiery floods by a new crater upon society. We are disposed to take the ground, therefore, on which alone the defects of the Mosaic legislation can be justified—that the hardness of men's hearts prevents a better system—and to inquire not what is the best possible law, but what are some of the features of a law that is at once desirable and feasible. It is a painful conviction which forces us into this position, a conviction, impressed by the history of divorce and divorce laws even in Christian civilization, that the strict rules of the New Testament cannot be introduced into our law, or if introduced, cannot long be enforced.*

A main feature of a good law will, of course, be to hold out no inducement to a husband or wife, who is dissatisfied with the present condition, to get a divorce, in order to contract a new alliance. Of course, the innocent party brings the petition or libel, and is able by forbearing to do so to prevent the other for an indefinite period from carrying out his or her purposes. And, of course the law-maker never intends to bring such a motive before the discontented consort. But the law offers in fact a premium for divorce whenever the disadvantages of such a step for the guilty party are inconsiderable. We maintain, therefore, in particular:

1. That the adulteress and the husband guilty of adultery ought never to be allowed to marry the partner in her or his crime. We are disposed to go farther and preclude the guilty wife, perhaps also the guilty husband, from contracting marriage with any person whatsoever, at least until the death of the innocent partner. In the *projet* of

* Comp. Stahl, Philos. d. Rechts II. 1, 364.

the *code civil*, as it came before the council of state, the adulteress could never marry again, and the guilty husband could never marry his concubine. M. Tronchet having said that this prohibition for the woman could have a dangerous influence on morals, by furnishing an excuse for future lewdness on her part, the law was amended so as to enact that the culpable party in cases of adultery could never marry his or her accomplice. (Art. 298.) We doubt the correctness of the conclusion while we admit that Tronchet has some reason for his opinion. Granting that some women thus branded by society will thus act, the question recurs whether it is worth while to save them at the expense of public virtue. Is it not better for society that such a woman lose her ordinary right by way of penalty—even as a citizen sometimes loses his right of office or of suffrage by fighting a duel or by bribery—than that the honorable state of the matron be degraded by her participation in its privileges. But, however this may be, we wonder that the law of England and a number of the United States should put nothing in the way of a divorced wife's marriage to her paramour. And this is the more strange in those codes which, like the law of Connecticut, impose the penalty of a long imprisonment upon persons guilty of adultery, while they permit such persons to marry whom they will the day after divorce has been decreed. The penalty is never inflicted, and the adulteress "wipeth her mouth" and takes the airs of an honest woman.

2. But again, adultery ought to be made penal —as it is in almost all the States, and provision should be made that the penalty should follow the sentence of divorce without any other trial. This suggestion will surprise some, perhaps, but it is simply borrowed from the *civil code.* (Art. 298, u. s.), "*La femme adultère sera condamnée par la même jugement—à la réclusion,*" *etc.* But the authors and revisers of that well-considered code did not contemplate a loose procedure like that which prevails among us, but a careful trial, and the same judgment which separated the parties was followed, simply on the requisition of the public officer, by the imprisonment of the woman.

So also in the project of a law of divorce in which Savigny had a part, it is provided that in decrees of divorce for cause of adultery, the punishment of the adulterous consort is to be pronounced, and also that the court is to find out the partakers in the crime as far as possible, and to hand over the evidence against such participators to the competent criminal court, as soon as the decree of divorce is passed.*

The question here arises whether adultery ought to have the same definition for the man and for the woman, and the same penalty, whichever

* Savigny, Vermischt. Schr. V., 378.

sex is guilty. According to all the ancient codes and many of the modern there is a distinction made between the sexes, and the distinction affects the law of divorce.* The crime is the same, except that it is justly regarded as a greater advance in wickedness for women as a class to be unfaithful in the marriage relation than for men. The harm done to society by such unfaithfulness is far greater for the woman, when her guilt is, so to speak, inside of the family, than when the father of the family commits the crime. There are strong reasons for making a discrimination in punishment against the woman, and we incline also to set up those limitations on divorce for a husband's adultery which appear, in the principle, in English law and the French civil code.

3. In all cases of divorce, where the blameworthy party is allowed to marry again, such marriage within a certain term ought to be made unlawful. This will render it necessary of course that the court decide, according to the evidence submitted, which of the partners is blameworthy, and it may happen that both are so in the same or in different degrees. The Prussian law requires such a decision. Among us, as outward specific acts are noticed almost exclusively, the parties can hardly share the civil blame, and the faulty party cannot have a decree in his favor,

* See what has been said in former chapters on the provision in Roman civil law, French and English law, etc.

with the *seeming* exception of cases where a wife deserts her husband on account of ill-treatment. But whoever can have the fault fastened on him ought to be forbidden to marry for a considerable period. According to the *code civil* this interval is three years in the case of divorce by mutual consent. Beyond question such enforced delay for a considerable period would act as a very powerful motive in favor of the good conduct of married parties. This is shown not only by the nature of the case, but by experience in the Rhenish Prussian districts under French law, where although divorce by mutual consent was allowed, only a very few cases of it occurred during thirty-six years. We believe that if parties divorced by the provisions of the omnibus clause in the law of Connecticut, could not marry again for two or three years, the number of divorces would be greatly lessened. Nay, if instead of that clause, the divorce by mutual consent were introduced into our code together with the French limitation above mentioned of three years, we should be much better off than we are now.

4. Separation from bed and board without dissolution of wedlock may be resorted to in some cases and as a temporary measure. This kind of separation was unknown to the ancients, and owes its origin to the Apostle's words—" but if she depart, let her remain unmarried or be reconciled to her husband,"—which refer, as we have given our

reasons for supposing, not to separation for the cause of adultery but for minor faults. Being consistent with the doctrine that marriage is indissoluble and is a sacrament of perpetual efficacy, it gradually superseded divorce *a vinculo* which involved the opposite doctrine. Since the decree of Gratian was compiled, that is from about the year 1150, the only separation known to the Catholic Church, and to Catholic countries fully obedient to its law, is from bed and board for a longer or shorter period: for life, it may be, in the case of a woman's adultery; for a time, on account of smaller offenses against the law of marriage. The feelings of the Catholics, trained up for centuries by their theory of the sacraments, ought to be respected in the legislation of a country where religions live side by side on an equal footing. Hence in every case where divorce is allowed by our laws, either the petitioner who gains his point ought to have liberty to choose separation *a mensa et toro*, or else the wishes of the two parties ought to determine in this respect. The latter appears in the present form of the *code civil:* "il sera libre aux époux de former demande en séparation de corps." The former was contained in the *projet* before it was amended: "L'époux qui aura le droit de demander le divorce pourra le borner à la demande en séparation de corps et des biens." We should unite the two in this way: if the parties can agree, the decree of the court may pronounce a separation instead of a divorce; if they cannot—as, for instance, in the case of mixed marriage—the petitioner or libeler may decide. For he, being the injured party, ought to have his choice; and he might have continued the state of marriage by taking no legal notice of the offense. But it is questionable whether his power to put a bar in the way of the other party ought to be perpetual.

But aside from those instances where religious scruples, fairly respected by the law, incline the parties to qualified separation, we cannot help feeling that this kind of divorce is liable to very grave objections. Such separation is only defensible on religious grounds, and if it prevailed in the law it would destroy the balance between the civil and the religious weight of marriage, throwing the former out of the scale altogether. The offended party has rights which he claims to have been invaded, and demands reparation. But the law refuses him reparation, in order that the offending party may be held to repentance. In no other case of wrong is such a principle admitted. But a still greater inconsistency with justice lies in this, that he is deprived for the future, it may be for his life, of an important right. He cannot marry again, because of the wrong done by his partner. It is like chaining a husband or wife to the corrupting body of a guilty consort executed by the law's sentence. It is, moreover, a source of great temptation. Let the sentence be that of lifelong separation for adultery, which prevents the innocent party from ever marrying another person, or forces the two to live together in a state of formal condonation, although the wrong has destroyed all affection. Is it likely that the majority of husbands would remain continent under that legal constraint, and cannot the toleration of concubinage in Catholic countries and the levity with which it is regarded be thus in part accounted for? And, still further, the same cause will lead people to make light of adultery, because the choice will be between a separation which has no effect on the marriage relation and a winking at the grossest violations of its sanctity? Will not the parties be tempted to think that to continue as they are, with the allowance to each other of leading no very strict life, is better than to make a noise about family matters, which can have no other effect than that of giving liberty to a married pair to live apart?

Such are some of the moral and jural difficulties attendant on separation from bed and board, when looked at as a general substitute for divorce. But the evils mentioned exist in but a slight degree when it is applied as a temporary measure for those less grievous offenses against the family constitution which do not preclude reconciliation. Cruelty and drunkenness, which are offenses, for the most part, of the husband, render the wife's state of life intolerable; desertion and crime, subjecting to a long imprisonment, break up the family state. But the violent man, the sot, the vagabond, the criminal, may be reformed: and what better school can he be in than that where he can feel himself to be repairing injuries and recovering the love of a wife and of children. Let the separation, then, be reserved for cases like these, as a temporary expedient, until it can be seen whether reform is to be hoped for. Only then, after a long enough probation, if there must be divorce, let the separation be turned into divorce on petition of the injured party. The Massachusetts law allows this substitution, or, in other words, permits remarriage, after five years from the passage of the decree, on application of the innocent party, and after ten years, on application of either party. In the *code civil*, power is given to the party who was originally the defendant, in all cases excepting where the complaint is against the woman for adultery, "to demand a divorce from the tribunal" after three years of separation. This permission given to the defendant, it is alleged, does no injury to the other's conscience, for although this act makes it free for him also to marry again, he may still consider himself bound by the law of his church.

5. The consequences of divorce, as it regards property, ought to be such that the injured party

shall sustain as little pecuniary loss or deficiency in the means of support as possible, and the culpable party shall be deprived of the benefits which the marriage or a marriage settlement placed within his or her reach. This was the great motive held out by Roman law, for although adultery was punishable from the time of Augustus, the penalty must have been rarely, if ever, inflicted, and divorce on other grounds enjoyed impunity. The arrangements in regard to this point are various in the different codes, and the adequate treatment of it would far transcend our limits. But the general principle is not only that the innocent and injured partner shall not lose the pecuniary advantages formerly derived from the connection, but also that, in gross cases at least, the offending party shall actually suffer in his goods on account of the wrong-doing. Something here must be left to the discretion of the court; but there ought to be some positive law directing and limiting that discretion.

6. The same may be said of the custody of the children, if there be any. The general principle here is that misconduct, which has broken up the family state and made light of all household endearments, shows unfitness to take charge of the children. They with the property sufficient for their maintenance must be intrusted to that one of the married pair who has been proved to be most regardful of the family interests, or, in case

of such a person's incompetence, to some third person.

7. The law ought to be specific and for determinate causes, and little discretion should be left in the hands of judges. To put the whole matter under the control of the judges without any specific legislation would, we are persuaded, be fruitful of evil. The judges would vary in their decrees—some granting divorce for slight grounds, others being more rigid. In such a country as ours, especially with an elected judiciary of short continuance, they might come to represent the public opinion, whatever it were, or there might be such a pressure of the bar upon them that they could not resist. Accordingly almost all our codes have been specific in their definitions of the causes justifying divorce, and have left but little freedom in the judge's hands. Few of our statutes indeed give the courts too great power. The great error consists in the allowance of divorce for indeterminate causes, although neither of the parties has committed any act that can be taken hold of. Such causes are incompatibility of temper and conduct which permanently affects the happiness of the marriage relation. We have already called the attention of our readers to the mischief which the "omnibus" clause has worked in the State of Connecticut. Such a law brings the judges oftentimes into extreme perplexity, for the happiness of the marriage relation is a very vague thing,

and a thing capable of being painted in very false colors by an interested party. It may be affected by great and small injuries, by unkind words, by lasting differences of policy in the management of children, or by a husband's refusal to give a wife money that she may dress ambitiously and above her rank. It adds strength, as Mr. Loomis observed in his Article, to other weak grounds of divorce. When a charge of habitual drunkenness or of failure to support is not sustained, this plea comes behind and props up a weak case. It tempts parties to marry improvidently, and opens the door through which they can escape from matrimony, for it amounts to not liking one another, and the dislike is enhanced by the prospect offered to the hopes of one or the other of making a more advantageous connection. Let the acts then be palpable on which a decree of divorce is based, and if the state of society is such that it shall seem desirable to separate parties on such vague grounds, let there be no dissolution, or at least no immediate dissolution of the marriage tie.

8. The procedure in petitions or libels for divorce needs a great change in many of the States, and the laws of the different States ought to be brought into a substantial uniformity. With regard to the first point we leave reforms to those who are better able to judge—to the better class of lawyers who have no interest in encouraging applications for divorce by looseness of procedure.

and who know what effect a change in practice is likely to have. But any one, lawyer or not, must be aware of the miserable state of things now existing in some of the States, and no one, who will compare the careful, thorough law of the *code civil* with most of our statutes relating to divorce, will feel any great respect for American legislation. Let us be allowed to illustrate the state of things by a single case occurring not a hundred miles from where we write. A woman had been married less than three months, when, on occasion of her making evening visits or a visit with a young man, her husband remonstrated, and high words took place. She left him, and earned her own living in another town. After about three months more she brought a petition for divorce, and the grounds alleged were adultery, habitual drunkenness, cruelty, and misconduct destroying domestic happiness. The three first the lawyer put in, it would seem, to strengthen his cause. The adultery was with a person unknown to the party complained of; habitual drunkenness was a false allegation, and had it been true, drunkenness for three months ought not to be regarded as habitual in the legal sense; cruelty he had scarcely a chance to commit. The man had, of course, a notice served on him, but, as we suppose, did not care to incur the expense, or to bring back to his house a woman whom he conceived to have injured him, and who did not want to keep him company. The divorce was allowed by the court. The woman apologized afterward for the charge of adultery, and said that the lawyer put it in. What went on the record we know not, but the records are so made up that many false charges appear on their pages.* We are persuaded not only that they are unreliable, but that they tend to give a false impression of the number of adulteries which are annually committed. When the judge thinks that possibly one or more higher offenses may have given cause for divorce, and that at all events the suit, if not the non-appearance of the party complained of, furnishes proof of bad relations in a household, he will be apt, if an omnibus clause permits it, to decide favorably upon the petition. And hasty examination of a case, with pressure of an interested lawyer, may not only break up a family, but put a permanent stamp on a man's or a woman's character.

It has been suggested that in *ex parte* proceed-

* We add *ex abundanti* an extract from a letter written by a legal gentleman in Indiana. [The seventh clause, to which reference is made, runs thus: "Any other cause for which the court shall deem it proper that a decree shall be granted."] It frequently happens, says that gentleman, "that the petition, which is not sworn to, contains several statutory cases, and perhaps also states facts which could only be the basis of a divorce under the seventh clause; and as the evidence is heard orally, and no record is kept of it, probably in not one in five of the records of divorces can the real ground of the divorce be obtained from the paper with certainty."

ings a state's attorney should *ex officio* be the guardian of the interest of the absent defendant. The laws of Indiana, where there are many such cases, strive to make their peace with justice and righteousness by thus protecting the absent party, but as the attorneys "have no acquaintance with the causes, their efforts are generally nominal."*

It would seem then that the laws ought to take greater care both of the absent defendant's interests and of him who is too poor to incur the expenses of the suit. We add that when the suit is not *ex parte*, and when the proceedings issue in a jury trial, divorce cases, at least on the complaint of adultery, ought to be secret—that is, no report of them ought to be allowed to appear in the public journals. The prurient curiosity of bystanders and the right of publicity do not weigh enough to counteract the interests of morality.

9. At the beginning of the proceedings, as well as in the course of them, attempts ought to be made by the magistrates to reconcile the parties, at least unless adultery be the thing complained of. This would involve a wide departure from our practice, which hurries onward toward an irrevocable decree.

* We use the words of the same gentleman whose opinion we have quoted in the last note.—Here we add that the Prussian project of a new law, already referred to, proposed to constitute an "Ehevertheidiger" or defender of marriage, whose duty it was to appear in all processes relating to divorce, invalidity or nullity of marriage, as the opponent of the party bringing the complaint.—Savigny u. s. v., 357.

The *code civil* by its delays favored reconciliation, and where divorce was desired by the joint consent of the parties, required the judges to make such exhortation to them, as would naturally lead them to abandon their project. The Prussian code again makes it imperative on the judges to attempt a reconciliation of the parties. But the project for the reform of that code, already referred to more than once, goes farther still. It proposes that no complaint shall be considered until the competent clergyman has certified that he has tried in vain to bring back the married pair to a state of peace. This may delay the case four months. Then, after the proceedings in the case are begun before the matrimonial court, the judges may institute new measures tending toward reconciliation "as often as they judge best, either directly or by commissioners, especially by the personal judge of the married pair, with or without clergymen called into council." Measures like these would not be suited to our state of society, but the principle must commend itself to all. And if in the course of time those valuable institutions, courts of arbitration or conciliation shall be introduced into any of the United States, they might be usefully employed on complaint of the aggrieved party to look into the case, to attempt to bring peace back into the household, and if that be impossible, to report to the judge whether there be *prima facie* ground for the petition for divorce.

The subject of divorce is complicated in this country by the number of jurisdictions and the ease of emigration. Just as a good paper currency was impossible when every State licensed its own banks, so it is with divorce laws. He who cannot get what he wants under the severe laws of New York, can become a free man by a short stay in Indiana. The validity of a divorce there need not, it is true, be always admitted by New York. Yet the facilities for such proceedings are among the worst parts of our system. Those who seek to reform the laws in this important article, will be bound to endeavor to stop those leaks which loose legislation in one State occasions everywhere else.

We have considered divorce legislation as immediately affecting the Christian Church, and as affecting society outside of the company of professed Christians. But for the interests of the Church of Christ it is not essential and absolutely necessary that the laws in this particular should be reformed. Indeed we may say that a greater facility of divorce than now exists, that even the allowance of divorce whenever the parties unite in desiring it, would assuredly awaken men of Christian principles to the evils of society; the discipline of the church would become stricter; and even in a country like ours, where Christians are no corporate or united body, but an aggregate of persons belonging to different, and often jealous denominations, where their joint action is almost out of the question, the evils of society, the greater they became, would the more rouse all those who bear the name of Christian to a common feeling, if not to concerted measures for their suppression. Christianity developed the purest principles of family life, and the noblest conception of marriage, in the midst of Greek and Roman society, where divorce was almost unrestrained, and under Jewish law, where, besides this freedom of divorce, polygamy was tolerated. And this it did before the sacramental theory was formed, and marriage regarded as one of the sacraments. So now, if they have any vitality, that is if they are really Christian, Christian communities can take care of themselves. "Do your worst then," we say, "in the matter of legislation. Make marriage in your codes a contract which the parties can dissolve at will, which either party can dissolve for very trifling reasons, which the State will dissolve for a great number of wrongs. Let your laws punishing adultery impose a penalty which nobody will mind, and let them be a dead letter. You but awaken then in the Christian communities an increasing sense of their responsibility as the guardians of morals; you only quicken in them the purpose to introduce within their own pales a stricter discipline, and to seek to leaven society more with their pure principles. Thus by your heathenish laws, you arouse the sensibilities of conscience and the instinct of self-preservation in a society which has immense power when once fairly in motion: you practically throw society into the hands of new legislators, and you will lead round a cycle of things, when your laws will give way to stricter ones, more consonant with the principles of morality, and when you will be looked upon as the enemies of social progress."

Greatly to be desired then as is a reform in divorce legislation, if the direct interests of religion are considered, it is not for this reason absolutely necessary, because the Christian Church can resist and counteract, and more than neutralize the existing laws, however bad they may be. But such reform is of immense importance, when we look at the effect of legislation on the general interests of society; when we look especially at those vast classes who, even in a country like ours, receive no direct influence from Christian truth and the Christian Church. What is to be done with and for the lower classes of society, in a country like ours, is one of the gravest of questions for the mind of a benevolent man. In a country which is mainly Protestant, the noblest things—the right of private judgment, and the intellectual light which always accompanies an open Bible—are a "savor of death" to the neglected classes: they are made self-confident, vain, uneasy, ready to receive the crudest falsehood, and to reject the most venerable truths. Religion appears to them a restraint, and religious people they are jealous of because these, in the natural order of things, get above them. So liberty also is another "savor of death" since they know not how to use their political right, fall into the hands of demagogues, and become, as a class, a political power within the State. Their cry is for freedom from restraint. Free rum, free Sundays, free suffrage, free divorce, and the like are their watchwords; and those who expect to get into power by their votes, are often afraid to contradict them, even if disgusted by their principles. What is to elevate or purify these classes? They stand aloof from the ennobling influences of religion; politics do not wash them clean; their "little learning is a dangerous thing;" their facilities for sensual gratification are less limited, perhaps, than those of the working class in any other land. There is no help for them, unless it lies in the voluntary movements of Christian enterprise, teaching the knowledge of Christ, and with it elevating the idea of family life. But loose divorce laws corrupt family life at its foundation, for it is hard for such persons to believe that what law sanctions is not right. Here then the conflict, between low views of marriage and divorce and the views contained in the New Testament, is waged to the greatest sacrifice of the interests of society. If one out of five or six of the marriages within a certain class is dissolved by law, and the law with the procedure in the courts almost offers a bribe to get rid of a husband or wife, how is family life to be sustained, how is it to have for that portion of the community its venerable or holy character? And the low conception of marriage tends to creep up into higher circles, as some of this class, from time to time, rise in respectability and wealth. Since, then, reforms in the divorce laws are especially needed for the lower stratum of society; since this class is most demoralized and corrupted by the fatal facility of the existing laws; and since it has in itself no power of self-recovery, when once thoroughly debased; it becomes all Christian and all benevolent persons, on their account mainly, to unite in an attempt to procure a reform in the laws concerning divorce, to bring legislation as near to the Christian standard as the people will bear.* We do not conceive that a reform in law would remove all the evils to which the marriage state is subject. Law cannot reform beyond a certain point, because "it is weak through the flesh." But bad law can corrupt even more than good law can purify.

But would not a strict divorce law defeat its own end? It certainly might, and that in two ways: first, by creating opposition enough to obtain an alteration of the law; and then, in a corrupt state of society, by tempting to sin within the marriage relation, if a person cannot free himself

* See Note 6, Appendix.

from its constraints. Yet it must not be supposed that, if divorce were confined to cases of adultery or at least to gross violations of marriage duties, such more flagrant crimes would be multiplied. This would be the case, if the law gave the adulterer the advantage of marrying again, but not if it took away the right from him or delayed the exercise of it for a term of years. And on the other hand loose divorce laws do not prevent adultery, as we have fully shown by the history of Roman society under the emperors.

We entertain no fear then that a system of divorce laws coming nigh—gradually, if it must be so—to the severity of the New Testament, will defeat its own end, and only force the corruptions of society into a worse channel. It is the defects of our present system that are corrupting. A system more in accordance with the idea of marriage could not, if accepted, fail to purify society.

APPENDIX.

NOTE 1 TO CHAPTER II.

On Certain Passages in the Epistles to Timothy and Titus.

THERE are certain passages in the first of Timothy and in Titus which have a possible bearing on divorce, and therefore may have a few words devoted to them in the present work. These passages are 1 Tim. iii. 2, 12; v. 9; Titus i. 6. The two first require the bishop or the deacon to be the husband of one wife; and the third makes it necessary, in order that a widow may receive the aid of the church, that she shall have been the wife of one husband. The expressions are precisely similar. It has been said, we are aware, that in the last passage the participle *γεγονυῖα* is to be joined with "one man's wife," and accordingly some editions of the Greek Testament put a comma after "sixty," which our version seems to favor by its rendering "having been the wife of one man." But such rendering violates the sense of *γεγονυῖα*, which could only mean "having become the wife of one man," which is nonsense. The participle is taken with the clause "not less than threescore years," and the sense is having come to be threescore years old. Exactly so Luke writes, ii. 42, "When he came to be (*ἐγένετο*) twelve years old," where we have the genitives again. And so in classical Greek. Plato says of his "master of education" (de leg. vi. 765 D.), "Let him have reached the age of not less than fifty years," *ἐτῶν γεγονὼς μὴ ἔλαττον ἢ πεντήκοντα.*

The passage in 1 Tim. v. 9, then, is like the others, and may be used to explain them. Two senses can be given to it. The first is that the widow must not have had more than one husband at a time. Now, as bald polyandry is not a thing to be conceived of, if such were the sense, it could only mean that there must not have been more than one person living at the same time, whose wife, according to the point of view of the author, or of Christians generally, she could have been called. In other words, she must not have been married to one husband while another was living. And so, after this analogy, we must explain "one woman's wife" to mean a man who could not be said, applying the Christian rule of marriage to him, to have more than one wife (that is, one person who can be called his wife) living. No one was to be allowed to say, that widow had two husbands at once, one a divorced, and one an actual husband; that elder has two wives, one dismissed and one living with him. But there is in our view a serious objection to this interpretation. We fall back therefore upon the second. The widow must be a *univira*, the elder or deacon a *monogamus*, in the sense in which that word (like *bigamus, digamus*) frequently occurs in the Christian Fathers, *i. e.*, one who never married the second time.

Now, why this rule of monogamy for the officers and widows? It was not given because the writer of the epistle thought second marriages unlawful, for he wishes to have the younger widows marry. Nor, secondly, was it given because he thought celibacy better than marriage for elders and deacons, for one must admit, as it seems to us, that the strain of his argument leads toward married elders rather than unmarried. For if an elder had governed his house well, it was a qualification for the eldership, but if he had not had any household, howcould his power of governing be known. Nor, thirdly, was it given because the pagans respected those who had married once, more than those who had married more frequently. It is true that a *univira*, a chaste widow, was held in honor as an example of virtue, but we do not find that the same rule was applied to men. Nor, finally, can he have had any ascetical tendency in giving out this rule. For this asceticism, in its forms of prohibition of marriage and abstinence from certain meats, is pointedly condemned in the fourth chapter of Timothy.

We can find no rule except one of these two, either that the *monogamy* and *monandry* gave *prima facie* evidence of restraint, or that a man or woman who had married twice or thrice would be more likely to have avoided those alliances which the Christian rule condemned, or, in other words, would be less likely to have put away a married partner, or to have taken one put away by another.

However we understand the passage, simultaneous polygamy cannot have been thought of.*

NOTE 2 TO CHAPTER III.

THE twenty-second novell of Justinian was repeated for the most part in the 117th, only in the latter the divorce *ex communi consensu* was expressly prohibited, as stated in the text. It served, with that succeeding novell, as the basis of subsequent legislation. The Basilicæ, says Walter, u. s., § 315, repeat literally the causes of divorce given in the novells of Justinian. We have no copy of this code in our hands, but have noticed in the manual or Hexabiblus of Harmenopulus, which has still authority in Greece, that the title on divorce is almost entirely borrowed from the source above mentioned. The freedom or rather laxity of divorce held its ground almost unchecked in the Eastern Church. It is remarkable; says Walter (u. s.), to see how Balsamon and other Greek canonists slip over the conflict of these laws with Scripture and tradition.

The twenty-second novell first made a discrimination between various kinds of divorce. The general statement (in chap. iv.) is this: "some marriages are dissolved during the life of the contractants *by the consent of the parties*, about which there is nothing that needs here to be said, since the parties arrange the

* Most recent interpreters and some of the Fathers explain these texts as we have done. Mathies and Huther, in Meyer's series, give a little different turn to them. The latter, on 1 Tim. iii. 2, makes the sense to be that the bishop has lived, or lives, with no woman in sexual intercourse except with his lawful wife.

affair as seems to them best, *others on a reasonable pretext* (κατὰ πρόφασιν εὔλογον, per occasionnem rationabilem), those namely which are called *bonâ gratiâ*, others again *without any cause*, and others still for a *reasonable cause*."

The *bonâ gratiâ* divorce is so named according to Wächter (die Ehescheid. bei den Röm., 223, u. s. w.), whose remarks we here to some extent adopt, for the first time in this novell. It stands between divorce by common consent and divorce on account of fault of one of the parties. It agrees with the first in this, that a certain sort of agreement of the parties is necessary, and with the other, that it is for determinate reasons. Its essential characters are the following: 1. No libellus repudii, it is probable, was necessary. 2. The divorced party was content, *i. e.*, did not oppose the transaction. 3. It was not obtained for crime, but for certain misfortunes of the divorced party. These were *impotence* for three years, from the time of marriage, instead of two years, as an earlier law had it (cap. 6); *captivity*, which according to the old jus postliminii dissolved marriage of course, even if the captive returned, but now was to continue for five years ere divorce could take place (cap. 7); *reduction to the state of slavery* by sentence of a judge, which could only happen in the case of a freedman (cap. 9); absence of the husband in the army for ten years to send any word to his wife or reply to her letters (cap. 14); which may be compared with a law of Constantine mentioned in our text; and the choice by either partner of a monastic life. In all the cases here mentioned except the last, each party takes back what property was brought by him or her into the partnership—the husband the antenuptial donation, the wife the *dos*. In the last case the party remaining in the world was to have whatever, according to the marriage contract, he or she was to have in the event of the death of the other (cap. v.). To these cases of *bonâ gratiâ* divorce Wächter adds sterility, not mentioned but in force before and not set aside by the novell.

The divorce for a good reason contains the same causes of divorce as the law of Theodosius II. referred to in the text, to which this novell adds three others against the woman: procurement of abortion, bathing with men wantonly, and taking steps to contract another marriage while living with her husband. In all these cases the innocent party has the *dos* and the antenuptial donation both. In no case where the woman is the innocent party is she permitted to marry again within a year (cap. 15, 16).

The only other feature of this law which we notice is the sanction given to marriages which were without *dos* or donation. If a man having married a woman on such terms expels her afterward from his house, he is required to pay over to her a fourth part of his substance—up to a hundred pounds of gold. Such marriages, being begun with no contract, would be regarded as unions with concubines, and so needed protection. (Cap. 18.) The dissolution of such marriages, however, *in fact* dissolved them *in jure*, so that the woman, if in fault, could yet marry after five years, while, if her husband was in fault for the divorce, she needed to wait only one year *propter seminis confusionem.*

In examining Roman legislation touching divorce, one cannot but be struck with the toughness of the old legislation, how hard it was to get it out of the old ruts, and what an uphill work it was for Christianity to convert and remodel law. Probably the difficulty was far greater than to infuse Christian ideas into a semi-barbarous people, and for this reason, among others, that the Roman looked on his system of law as something majestic and imperial. Yet a mean idea lay at the bottom of marriage. Money was its soul. *Dos* and *donatio ante* or *propter nuptias* play their part until one gets disgusted.

The late distinguished Frenchman, Troplong, in his excellent essay on the Influence of Christianity on Manners in the Roman Empire, devotes a number of pages to the subject of divorce. Prof. C. Schmidt, of Strasburg, takes up the same subject in his admirable essay which won a prize from the French Academy. But the results are not very satisfactory. Beyond all question, Christianity purified the conception of marriage among Christian believers, and the influence of the idea extended somewhat through society and naturally influenced legislation. But in the matter of divorce it encountered old habits which resisted it with an immense obstinacy, and so from Constantine onward we see divorce legislation swinging to and fro as if the two forces could never consent to any stable equilibrium. The most striking instance of this—we believe that we have not mentioned it elsewhere—is furnished by a novell of Justin II.—the 140th. After Justinian had abolished and made penal divorce by joint consent,—divorce, *bonâ gratiâ*, as this novell by an abuse of terms calls it,—this foolish emperor brings it back again, basing his alteration of the law of his predecessor on the quarrels which grew up between husband and wife. "For if," it is there said, "the state of feeling of the parties creates marriage, with reason the contrary disposition dissolves it by consent of the parties." Which proves too much, for the loss of love of one only ought, on those premises, to bring it to an end. This novell of A. D. 566 was set aside by the subsequent divorce laws of the Basilicæ.

NOTE 3 TO CHAPTER III.

Some Notices of Divorce Laws in the Middle Ages.

THERE are numerous proofs that the strict rule of the indissolubility of marriage met with obstacles in its way toward universal recognition. The laws of the Germanic and Scandinavian nations were, as might be expected, at first willing to grant absolute divorce on a variety of grounds; Roman law had some influence on barbarian law in this direction, after the breaking up of the empire; and in some countries the ecclesiastical synods were willing to tolerate departures from the church rule already tolerably well established.

We propose, in this note, to give a few brief illustrations of the state of things in regard to divorce, while the Church of the West was undertaking to bring about a uniformity of practice.

In the strictly heathen state of these nations, divorce would have been allowed for a variety of reasons besides the wife's adultery. The causes might be, by Icelandic usage, such as the husband's cowardice, unseemly demeanor of either, or discord or maltreatment of the parents of either party by the other, or impotence, or, it would seem, even poverty. Discord and malicious desertion continued to justify divorce after Christianity was known, but the bishop alone could dissolve the connection. (See Gans, Erbrecht, iv., 489 ff.)

In the laws of Aethelbirht of Kent (A. D. 560–616), it is said that "if a free man lieth with a freeman's wife he shall purchase her with her (or his) wergild, and get another wife out of his own property and bring her home to the other man." (R. Schmid, Gesetz. d. Angels, 2d ed., p. 5, No. 31.) In another law, No. 79, it is said that if "she will depart with children she shall have half the property," from which Gans (iv. 299) argues that separation was tolerably free.

In the Burgundian laws it is said of a woman putting away her husband *necetur in luto.* A man is authorized to dismiss his wife for adultery, poisoning, and robbing of graves only, where we trace the influence of Roman law. If he does this for other reasons he must either pay "alterum tantum quantum pro pretio ipsius dederat (*i. e.* the wife-price or morgengabe), besides a mulct of twelve solidi, or must leave his house and property to his children and move away. (Gans, iv., 36.)

Among the Lombards the stricter law of divorce was fully introduced by Charlemagne and Lothair. Before the conquest by the Franks fines for divorce appear. King Grimoald ordained that if a married man took another wife he should pay 500 solidi and lose the guardianship over his first.* (Gans, iii., 180.)

In the formulas in use among the Franks there are signs of divorces quite contrary to the rules of the church. A formula of Marculf (ii., 30, Walter's Corpus, iii.), it is said that the marriage is dissolved because there is no love according to God's will between the parties, but discord. And they are free either to go into a convent or to marry again. (Gans, iv., 83.)

In the Westgothic laws divorce is permitted only in the case of adultery—indeed it was the consequence of this offense, as the adulterer and the guilty wife ceased to be free, and became the property of the injured party. Earlier usages permitted divorce by consent. "Let no one presume," a law had it, "to join in marriage to himself a free woman divorced from her husband, unless either by writings or before witness the fact shall be

* Grimoaldi leges, vi., in Walter's Corpus, i., 756.

evident that a divorce took place." But such divorces were afterward forbidden by King Chindasuintha, and adultery now constituted the only ground of divorce. See Gans, u. s., iii., 341–344.

As we have seen that the church temporized among the Scandinavians, so was it more or less elsewhere. Among the Anglo-Saxons the Pœnitentiale of Egbert of York, (?) belonging to the middle of the eighth century, shows that the wife's—but not the husband's—adultery, impotence, desertion, and captivity furnished grounds for divorce, with remarriage, of which the church in England admitted the validity. (Phillips, Angelsächs., Recht., p. 243.) The old British church seems to have had stricter rules. In France, during the eighth century, things were, if any thing, still looser. Richter affirms (Kirchenr. § 282, note 7), that *mutual consent* was there a reason for divorce, and at least in two cases remarriage of one or both parties could follow, namely, when a vow of chastity was taken by one of the parties, and when one became leprous. Furthermore, the following reasons, emanating *from one of the parties*, justified divorce: adultery, desertion of a wife, a husband's crime punished with servitude, captivity of either party, plotting against the other's life, change of rank from slavery to freedom, refusal of connubial duty, impotence, and even supervenient impotence. The decree of Gratian has the following sentence of Greg. III., (A. D. 731–740): "Si mulier infirmitate correpta non valuerit debitum viro reddere—ille qui se non poterit continere nubat magis," etc. The capitulum of the synod of Vermerie under Pippin, A. D. 752, permitting divorce with marriage to a man, against whose life his wife has conspired with others, we have spoken of before. Another article of the capitulary of the same assembly agrees with the above-mentioned sentence of Gregory III. Five years afterward, in the meeting at Compiègne (Compendium), it was enacted (capit. 16), that either husband or wife might separate from the other, being leprous, and marry whom he or she would.*

All this shows the conflict of expiring Roman with ecclesiastical law. We have noticed a still later instance in the *assises des*

* Some of these statements Catholic writers seek to explain away.

bourgeois of the kingdom of Jerusalem (§ 155, p. 322, ed. Foucher): "Sometimes it happens"—it is there said—"that a man takes a wife, and this woman then becomes leprous, or has the falling sickness badly (ou chiet de mauvais mal trop laidement), or her mouth or nose sends forth a very offensive odor (ou il put trop dure la bouche ou le nés)," etc. In such cases, reason requires that the church ought to separate them, and accordingly, after proof of the fact, the unfortunate woman is to be put into a convent (soit rendus en religion), and the husband can then take another wife. The wife can do the same when similar misfortunes befall the husband. Then follows a rule for the paying over of her dower to the abbess of the convent, etc. This is remarkable, considering that it contradicts the canon law in the thirteenth century, and yet the less remarkable when we consider the rule of Gregory above cited, which furnishes a precedent.

Our limits forbid us to speak of the penalties which the laws of the Germanic and earlier barbarous kingdoms attach to adultery. We must refer for that subject to Wilda's Strafrecht d. Germanen, pp. 821–829.

NOTE 4 TO CHAPTER IV.

Foljambe's Case.

In the present note we shall follow, for the most part, the late Prof. Craik, of Belfast, Ireland, who, in the Appendix to the Romance of the Peerage, Vol. I., cited in our text, has submitted this case to an accurate examination, and has shown the mistakes of previous writers.

Mr. Bishop, in his work on marriage and divorce (i., § 661, 4th ed.), says that "anciently, judicial divorces were probably from the bond of matrimony. But in 1601 a contrary rule was, in the Court of Star Chamber, established by Whitgift, archbishop of Canterbury, assisted by other eminent divines and civilians." His authority is Foljambe's case, reported in 3 Salkeld, 137. And again, in § 705, he reaffirms the same thing, but without proof, saying only that the fact is now generally admitted.

That sentences of nullity in ecclesiastical courts dissolved marriage, or, more properly, declared it never to have existed, is known to all. But there is not the slightest evidence that these courts gave a license to marry another person in any other case. They could not have done it in the old Catholic times, and no other courts had jurisdiction over marriage and divorce. Nor has any evidence been produced that after the Reformation—however, some may have married a second wife while the first was living, feeling no dread of the censures which were only ecclesiastical—the case was altered.

The note in Salkeld's Reports, which has misled the author of the article on divorce in the Penny Cyclopædia and a number of others, including Mr. Bishop, is as follows: "A divorce for adultery was anciently *a vinculo matrimonii*, and therefore, in the beginning of the reign of Queen Elizabeth, the opinion of the Church of England was, that after a divorce for adultery the parties might marry again; but in Foljambe's case, *Anno* 44 Eliz., in the Star Chamber, that opinion was changed; and Archbishop Bancroft, upon the advice of divines, held that adultery was only a cause of divorce *a mensa et toro*."

Salkeld wrote in the early part of the eighteenth century, and, as Prof. Craik shows, makes two errors, besides mistaking the main fact. One of these is that Bancroft was primate in 44 Eliz., or 1601, whereas Whitgift lived until 1604; and the other, that the Star Chamber, a court which had no jurisdiction in such cases, and where "the archbishop neither sat alone nor presided," should have rendered such a decision.

But we may go back to Moore's Reports of the seventeenth century, in which, as indeed in Noy's Reports (1656), the matter of Foljambe is thus stated. We translate from the law French. "Feb. 13, *anno* 44 Eliz. In the Star Chamber it was declared by all the court, that whereas (?) Fuljambe was divorced from his first wife for the incontinence of the woman, and afterward had married Sarah Page, daughter of Rye, in his former wife's lifetime, this was a void marriage, was only *a mensâ et thoro*, and not at all *a vinculo matrimonii*. And John Whitgift, then archbishop of Canterbury, said that he had called to himself at Lambeth the most sage divines and civilians, and that they had all agreed therein."

Here the darkness begins to clear up. It is Whitgift, not Bancroft, who was concerned in the affair, and the primate had held a council, not a court, at his palace. But there remains the fact that, somehow or other, Foljambe's marriage had come before the Star Chamber, of which Whitgift was a member. A natural explanation might be in this, that this point was only incidental to the main issue before the court.

The registers of this court perished with it, or at least are not now to be found, but Mr. Craik hunted up in the Chapter House some of the depositions taken in this case. From these it appears that Hercules Foljambe, Esq., *defendant* in the case, had been divorced for his own adultery from two wives, and while they were alive had married a third, Mrs. Sarah Page, a widow, the daughter of the complainant, Edward Rye, of Misterton. The complaint was that Foljambe, in right of his so-called wife, had seized the manor-house of Misterton, held by lease of the Chapter of York Cathedral, and had by force kept out Rye, on the claim that not Rye but his daughter was the lessee. The wrong charged against Foljambe was this illegal exclusion of Rye, claiming to be the rightful tenant, and the disturbance which he had thus excited. On this alone, says Mr. Craik, could the court give judgment, but "it is likely enough that, in so aggravated a case, the illegality of the defendant's pretended marriage with the daughter of the complainant, his only plea, may have been strongly pointed out and denounced. But to quote this case as establishing any thing new is absurd, and almost equally so whether the decision be taken to have been that of the archbishop (as seems to be not an uncommon notion), or that of the court of the Star Chamber. No judgment of either the one or the other upon such a question could have carried with it any authority whatever."

The facts, then, when sifted, seem to be these: 1. Foljambe, like many others in Elizabeth's reign, feared no penalties of the common or statute law for his audacious marriage, for there were none, and cared nothing for those of the law ecclesiastical. 2. The validity of his marriage came up incidentally. 3. The primate, in consequence of the loose state of opinion, thought it best to take the *consilia prudentum* touching divorce, and submit them to the court. 4. The law of England had remained unaltered. 5. It is not improbable that this gross case, belonging to Feb., 1602, may have led to the new canons and new statute of the first year of James I., a little more than a year after.

NOTE 5 TO CHAPTER V.

Extract from Rev. H. Loomis' article on Divorce Legislation in Connecticut. New Englander for July, 1866.

DURING a period of fifteen years nearly 4,000 divorces have been granted; a number equal to one-twentieth of all the families in the State. Are we not justified in the conclusion that the law of 1849 effected not merely a change, but a revolution in the legislation of the State in the matter of divorce! How then has this revolution been accomplished? If we turn again to the terms of that law we find that three new causes of divorce were added by it—imprisonment for life, infamous crime, and general misconduct. Applications for divorce, for the first two of these causes, occur but seldom in the records of the courts, and cannot, from the nature of the case, have affected materially the whole number granted. It is to the third cause, therefore, that we must look for the multiplication fivefold of the decrees of divorce by our courts, and yet by reference to a classified table subjoined, in which the decrees of divorce for the year 1864, and two months of 1865, are given in connection with their causes, it appears that only one-sixth of the whole were granted expressly for general misconduct alone. It is, indeed, exceedingly curious to notice the effect which this so-called general misconduct clause has had upon the construction of the entire enactment, of which it forms apparently so subordinate a part. It is noticed sometimes in musical instruments that an attachment directly connected with but a portion of the scale, and designed primarily to affect but the notes of a single octave, is found in practice to give a new tone and character to the whole instrument throughout its entire range. Something analogous to this would seem to have been the effect of this general misconduct attachment to our divorce law. Its influence has been felt, not only in the suits brought specifically in its name, but in extending the loose, vague, and indefinite character of its own terms over the language and administration of the entire enactment. In addition to the tables carefully prepared for that purpose it may not be improper to introduce in this connection other parts of the evidence laid before the special committee appointed by the Legislature of 1865 to take into consideration, and report upon the recommendation of the Governor, in relation to a reform in our laws of divorce. In the evidence presented to that committee, from which are drawn almost all the facts quoted in this article in regard to the present administration of our divorce law, was the opinion of two of our judges who have recently retired from the bench, that of the 4,000 divorces granted in this State during the past fifteen years, more than half have been secured through the influence, direct or indirect, of this general misconduct clause.

In a vast number of cases, in which the evidence in reference to the particular offense alleged in the suit must have been rejected as insufficient, the additional claim urged by counsel, that "the happiness of the petitioner had been destroyed, and the end of the marriage relation defeated," has been sufficient to secure a decree of divorce. In fact it may be said that the indirect influence of this clause has been far greater than any it could independently have secured; and where upon this issue alone a decree could not have been obtained, yet, coupled with the charge of adultery, though amounting to only a suspicion—or with desertion for a shorter period than provided for in the statute; or with evidence of intemperance and cruelty, which would be held wholly insufficient in itself as a ground of divorce—this plea of general misconduct has, in innumerable instances, been pressed to an actual decree. Indeed, when we consider the indefinite terms of this provision, it is difficult to set any limit to the amount of pressure which may be brought, by interested friends, to bear upon the mind even of the most conscientious judge, to induce a dissolution of the relationship. The whole matter is, in effect, placed under his almost absolute discretion; and where the State has intrusted such almost unlimited power over the most sacred relation of life, with few and slight limitations or barriers of any kind to preserve it from abuse, it need not surprise us to find at least equal laxity in its practical exercise. Apart, however, from the loose language of the statute, and the large discretion allowed to the judge, it would be difficult to conceive of any thing called a court, constituted with more inevitable tendency to dangerous laxity of practice than the Superior Court extemporized, during the few minutes just before or after one of its ordinary sessions, into a Court of Divorce.

But whatever may be said of the constitution of the court, its usages are certainly such as are known to no other court, civil or criminal, high or low, within the jurisdiction of the State. Not only is it true in nine cases out of ten, or more exactly, as our second table shows, in ten cases out of eleven, that there is no appearance whatever for the respondent, and consequently all the evidence presented is *ex parte*, but it is a notorious fact that, ordinarily, no sufficient measures are complied with to secure notice to the respondent. It is true the law provides that certain parties may issue an order of notice, but what the order shall be, and what the evidence of its service, are left again to the discretion of the officer who issues it, and practically the duty is fulfilled, as shown in the evidence before the committee, by the discharge of a letter through the post-office to the last address which the petitioner who brings the suit may choose to furnish.

Whether, in the etiquette of a Court of Divorce, it be considered discourteous or otherwise, to the lawyer prosecuting a divorce suit, for the judge to submit the witnesses provided to any very close examination, direct or indirect; and whether in a Court of Divorce the assurance of a lawyer as to what he *can* prove is equivalent to the actual proof itself or not, it is certain that the hearing of quite a batch of divorce suits in the half-hour between the closing of the morning session of the court and the time for dinner does not ordinarily involve any risk of a cold repast on the part either of the court or the witnesses.

NOTE 6 TO CHAPTER VI.

THAT divorce laws, by great laxity, and by allowing criminal attachments of married persons to result in a new marriage between the guilty parties, must undermine family virtue, and put it into the heads of people to get divorces who would otherwise have lived in peace, all will admit. On the other hand, severe divorce laws no more tend to multiply adultery and other high offenses against the family state than lax ones, as we seem to have shown. But the influence of law is limited. No one supposes that a good divorce law will do more than abridge the number of flagrant offenses against marriage. If adultery is punished instead of being rewarded, there will be fewer instances of this crime; while loose laws, like those of Rome under the empire, where divorce by agreement or by action of one of the parties was exceedingly easy, and concubinage was allowed, did not diminish the higher crimes, although adultery was punishable. We look, then, beyond law to the idea of marriage, as the gospel presents it to us, and to moral and religious training for the preservation of the sanctity of marriage in a nation, anxious only that the law do not pour its great influence in another direction.

But nations differ in their proclivities. Some, it would seem, run more into one form of evil, and others into another. So the form of civilization may encourage divorce. We might count among the causes of unhappy marriages among us, connected with our national character and civilization, anxiety and want of light-heartedness making home cheerless and leading to drink; the equality of condition which makes the poor, especially in the matter of the dress of females, emulate the rich; the nervous irritability and love of excitement of the nation, induced in part by our climate; the trashy food of paltry novels by which false imaginations of matrimonial life are nurtured; the tendency toward material enjoyments; the haste in forming connections arising out of the ease with which life is sustained; the general freedom of choice and movement which makes law a yoke, while habits of thrift, self-restraint, and endurance have in part lost their old power.

It is an important inquiry for the social philosopher, how far frequency of divorce is, at its root, connected with other social evils. For instance, within a few years many voices have been lifted up to proclaim that a frightful sin—that of preventing the increase of families by methods of abortion, and in other base ways—is becoming rife among us. Dr. Allen, in eastern Massachusetts, seeks to show this, and Bishop Cox, in eastern New York, warns his flock, in a pastoral letter, against "ante-natal infanticide." The crimes are the crimes of native Americans and of so-called Protestants, not of those foreign Catholics against whom men blow the trumpet of alarm. It is impossible that there should not be a foundation for these imputations: the evidence for them meets us too plainly to be denied, although the argument from the decrease in the size of families is not a conclusive one. But our point here is, how much is divorce connected with such a vice as this? Must not the same want of recognition of the true ends of marriage lead to this and to divorce. A heathenized mind is seen in both. Nay, a mind worse than that of some heathens, of the ancient Germans, for instance, among whom "*numerum liberorum finire flagitium habetur.*" And what is the cause of this unwillingness to have a family? Is it dread of expense, or trouble? Are children no longer regarded as a blessing? And if they are thus prevented from coming into the world, is not divorce the more unimpeded? Or is the fearful selfishness shown in such deliberate sin likely to bind the marriage pair together? But we pursue the subject no further, only adding that the same religious and moral teaching, and the same healthy laws that oppose divorce, must tend to put a stop to this crime also.

INDEX.

The references are to the pages. C denotes cited.

A.

13*

B.

C.

D.

E.

F.

G.

H.

I. J.

K.

L.

M.

N.

O.

P.

R.

U.

V.

CHARLES SCRIBNER. A. C. ARMSTRONG. A. J. PEABODY.

Condensed Catalogue

OF THE PUBLICATIONS OF

CHARLES SCRIBNER & CO.,

654 BROADWAY,

NEW YORK. JANUARY, 1868.

*** *The figures in the last column of this Catalogue refer to* CHARLES SCRIBNER & CO.'S *Descriptive Catalogue, copies of which will be sent to any address upon application.*

*** *Blanks in the column of prices, except in the case of School Text-Books, the prices of which may be learned from* CHARLES SCRIBNER & CO.'S *Educational Catalogue, indicate that the Works are either out of print or in press.*

*** *In this list the names of Books just published are given in* SMALL CAPITALS; *those issued during the year* 1867, *as well as new editions of Works previously produced, are indicated by italics.*

*** *The prices here given are for the regular style of binding in cloth. Books furnished in other styles, and their respective prices, may be learned from the Descriptive Catalogue.*

*** *Any of these Books will be sent post-paid to any address upon receipt of the price.*

	Volumes.	Size.	Price.	Page
ADAMS, W., D.D.				
THANKSGIVING	1	12mo	$2 00	2
Three Gardens	1	12mo	2 00	1
AGASSIZ, PROF. LOUIS.				
Structure of Animal Life (The)	1	8vo	2 50	2
ALEXANDER, A., D.D.				
Moral Science	1	12mo	1 50	3
ALEXANDER, J. W., D.D.				
Alexander, Archibald, Life of, (Portrait)	1	12mo	2 00	3
Christian Faith and Practice (Discourses)	1	12mo	2 00	6
Consolation (Discourses)	1	12mo	2 00	5
Faith (Discourses)	1	12mo	2 00	6
Forty Years' Correspondence with a Friend	2	12mo	4 00	4
Preaching, Thoughts on	1	12mo	2 00	5

	Volumes.	Size.	Price.	Page.
ALEXANDER, J. A., D.D.				
Acts (Commentary)	2	12mo	$4 00	8
Isaiah " (complete)	2	8vo	6 50	7
" " (abridged)	2	12mo	4 00	8
Mark "	1	12mo	2 00	8
Matthew "	1	12mo	2 00	8
Psalms "	3	12mo	6 00	7
New Test. Literature and Ecc. Hist. . .	1	12mo	2 00	9
Sermons (with Portrait)	2	12mo	——	9
ALLSTON, WASHINGTON.				
Lectures and Poems	1	12mo	2 50	9
ANDREWS, REV. S. J.				
Life of Our Lord	1	post 8vo	3 00	10
ARMSTRONG, G. D., D.D.				
Works of	3	12mo ea.	1 25	11
BAUTAIN, PROF. A.				
Extempore Speaking	1	12mo	1 50	12
BEECHER, REV. H. W.				
PRAYERS FROM PLYMOUTH PULPIT . .	1	12mo	1 75	13
BOTTA, PROF.				
Dante as Poet, Patriot, Philosopher . .	1	crown 8vo	2 50	14
BRACE, CHARLES L.				
Hungary, with Experience of Austrian Police,	1	12mo	——	15
Home Life in Germany	1	12mo	——	14
Norse Folk	1	12mo	2 00	15
Races of Old World	1	post 8vo	2 50	15
Short Sermons for Newsboys	1	16mo	1 50	16
BUSHNELL, HORACE, D.D.				
Character of Jesus	1	18mo	1 00	19
Christ and his Salvation	1	12mo	2 00	19
Christian Nurture	1	12mo	2 00	18
Nature and the Supernatural	1	12mo	2 25	17
New Life, Sermons for	1	12mo	2 00	19
Vicarious Sacrifice, The	1	8vo	3 00	18
Work and Play	1	12mo	2 00	19
CHEEVER, G. B., D.D.				
Works of	3	12mo	——	20
CLARK, PROF. N. G.				
English Language, Elements of	1	12mo	1 25	21
COLLIER, J. PAYNE, F.S.A.				
Rarest Books in English Language . .	4	small 8vo	12 00	21
CONYBEARE, REV. W. J., and HOWSON, REV. J. S.				
St. Paul, Life and Epistles of (illustrated)	2	8vo	7 50	22

	Volumes.	Size.	Price.	Page.
COOK, PROF. J. P., JR.				
Religion and Chemistry	1	crown 8vo	$2 50	24
CRAIK, GEO. L., LL.D.				
English Literature and Language . .	2	8vo	7 50	23
CROSBY, PROF. HOWARD, D.D.				
New Testament with Notes	1	12mo	1 50	24
CRUMMELL, REV. A.				
Africa, Future of.	1	12mo	1 00	—
DANA, A. H.				
Ethical and Physiological Inquiries . .	1	12mo	1 50	25
DANA, R. H.				
Poems and Prose Writings.	2	12mo	4 00	25
DAWSON, HENRY B.				
Fœderalist (Univ. Ed.)	1	8vo	3 00	25
" with Notes	1	8vo	3 75	25
DAY, PROF. H. N.				
ENGLISH COMPOSITION	1	12mo	1 50	26
DISCOURSE, (Rhetoric)	1	12mo	1 50	26
Logic	1	12mo	1 50	27
DERBY, EDWARD, EARL OF.				
Homer's Iliad (translated)	2	crown 8vo	5 00	28
DE VERE, M. SCHELE, LL.D.				
Studies in English	1	crown 8vo	2 50	29
DINGMAN, J. H.				
Publisher's Sheet-Book	1	Folio	15 00	29
DRUMMOND, REV. JAS.				
Christian Life, Thoughts for	1	12mo	1 50	30
DUYCKINCK, E. A. and G. L.				
Cyclopædia of Am. Literature (400 Portraits, &c.)	2	royal 8vo	10 00	31
DWIGHT, BENJ. W.				
Philology, Modern	2	8vo	6 00	30
ELLET, MRS. E. F.				
American Revolution, Domestic History of	1	12mo	1 50	32
" " Women of . .	3	12mo	——	33
Pioneer Women of the West	1	12mo	1 50	32
QUEENS OF AM. SOCIETY (13 steel engravings)	1	12mo	2 50	33
ELLIOTT, CHARLES W.				
New England History.	2	8vo	6 00	34
EWBANK, THOS.				
Hydraulics	1	8vo	6 00	34
FELTER, S. A.				
Arithmetics, Natural Series of	1	——	——	35-36

	Volumes.	Size.	Price.	Page.
FIELD, HENRY M., D.D.				
Atlantic Telegraph, History of	1	12mo	$1 75	37
FISHER, REV. PROF. GEO. P.				
Supernatural Origin of Christianity . .	1	8vo	2 50	38
Silliman, Benj., LL.D., Life of (Portrait)	2	crown 8vo	5 00	37
FORSYTH, WM.				
Cicero, New Life of (Illustrations) . .	2	crown 8vo	5 00	35
FOWLER W. C., LL.D.				
Sectional Controversy (The)	1	8vo	1 75	39
FROUDE, J. A.				
HISTORY OF ENGLAND	10	crown 8vo	3 00 ea.	40
SHORT STUDIES ON GREAT SUBJECTS . .	1	crown 8vo	3 00	41
GAGE, REV. W. L.				
Carl Ritter, Life of	1	12mo	2 00	42
GASPARIN, COUNT.				
America before Europe	1	12mo	2 00	42
GIBBONS, J. S.				
PUBLIC DEBT OF THE UNITED STATES .	1	crown 8vo	2 00	43
GUIZOT, M.				
Meditations (First and Second Series) .	2	12mo	ea. 1 75	43
GUYOT, PROF. ARNOLD.				
Geographies, Wall Maps, Key, etc. . .	-	——	——	44-47
HALL, EDWIN, D.D.				
Puritans and their Principles	1	8vo	2 50	48
HALSEY, REV. LEROY J.				
Bible, Literary Attractions of	1	12mo	1 75	48
HEADLEY, J. T.				
Complete Works of	15			49-53
HEIDELBERG,				
Catechism	1	small 4to	3 50	54
HERBERT, H. W.				
Works of	3	12mo	ea. 1 50	54
HOLLAND, DR. J. G. (Timothy Titcomb.)				
Bay-Path. A Novel	1	12mo	2 00	58
Bitter-Sweet. A Poem	1	12mo	1 50	56
Gold Foil	1	12mo	1 75	56
KATHRINA. A Poem	1	12mo	1 50	59
Lessons in Life	1	12mo	1 75	57
Letters to the Joneses	1	12mo	1 75	57
Letters to Young People	1	12mo	1 50	55
Miss Gilbert's Career	1	12mo	2 00	59
Plain Talks on Familiar Subjects . . .	1	12mo	1 75	58

www.ingramcontent.com/pod-product-compliance
Lightning Source LLC
LaVergne TN
LVHW020228110826
845151LV00003B/857

* 9 7 8 1 4 2 5 5 3 1 7 7 5 *